High Shelf

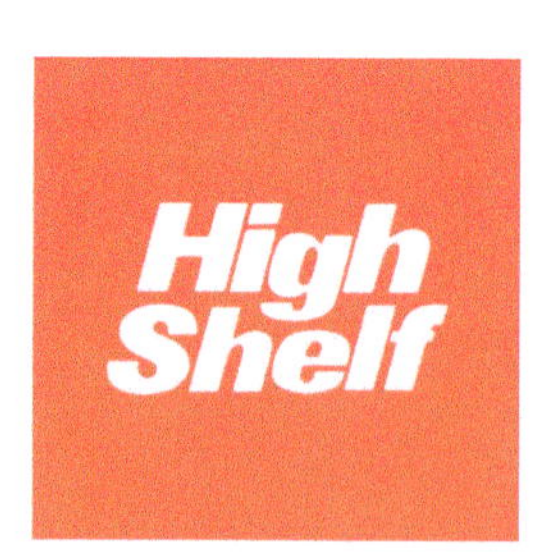

High Shelf Issue XVI, March 2020
Portland, Oregon.
Copyright 2020, High Shelf Press

ISBN: 978-1-7342842-7-0

Cover Image by Christine Friedman
Design and Layout by C. M. Tollefson
Edited by David Seung & C. M. Tollefson

High Shelf XVI

March 2020

"Remember climbing trees?

Hands sticky with pitch,
ripped jeans. Spine
curved into a crook… "
                              Gina Williams

"... I meant to make a place
for us and call it elsewhere.
where you could train your eyes
skyward to the overhang of leaves

and soften your eyes and soften your body and give..."
Danielle Vermette

Table Of Contents

new here

Margaret Galey

(1)

I want it to always be this good
 I'm drawing a map to
    stay   *say*   s l o w e r now
you've had more practice

 reclaim stories from
another day   *breathe*
   I'm listening &
  can't imagine but

        yes&no&yes
your realsouthernmanners
 oh honestly now
I know the secret

let's break some windows
I'd better not
      how does this work?
how does this even work ?

[breathless]
 it's been awhile
I'm listening
    shhh breathe

I nap with abandon I'm
abrokenoffpage &
new here but
        I'm listening .

(2)

wetgrassmornings
 s o v e r y c l o s e
take it off already
you've had more practice

boozy redcarpetwetdream
    I'm new here
how does this work ?
laugh it off already

I take my time
break it off already
[breathless]
            how

 does this even work ?
KentuckyWoodsongsRadio
& backseamtattoos
mmm   it's been awhile

backyard homebase &
 awkward routes   call
   it quits   fadeto
          blackout.

Openings
Danielle Vermette

I meant to make a painting
of the womb in you.
To convey the heat
of your new want with color.

I meant to carry a swarm
of fireflies to you
to lend a soft glow to
the cave of your quiet.

I meant to trust my mouth
to open again. To believe
in openings, to believe a person
can become and keep on becoming.

I meant to want
to live in the sunshine,
instead of where the outside
storms match the inside weather.

I meant to make a place
for us and call it elsewhere.
where you could train your eyes
skyward to the overhang of leaves

and soften your eyes and soften your body and give
into your body and give of your body
and from your body, see you are

the same as I
the same as I

I meant to tell better stories
and take up all the space
in the room, to be as big as the house
like he is, to be bigger than the house

I meant for you to never doubt
your place in me.

Quiet Amok

Olivia Djawoto

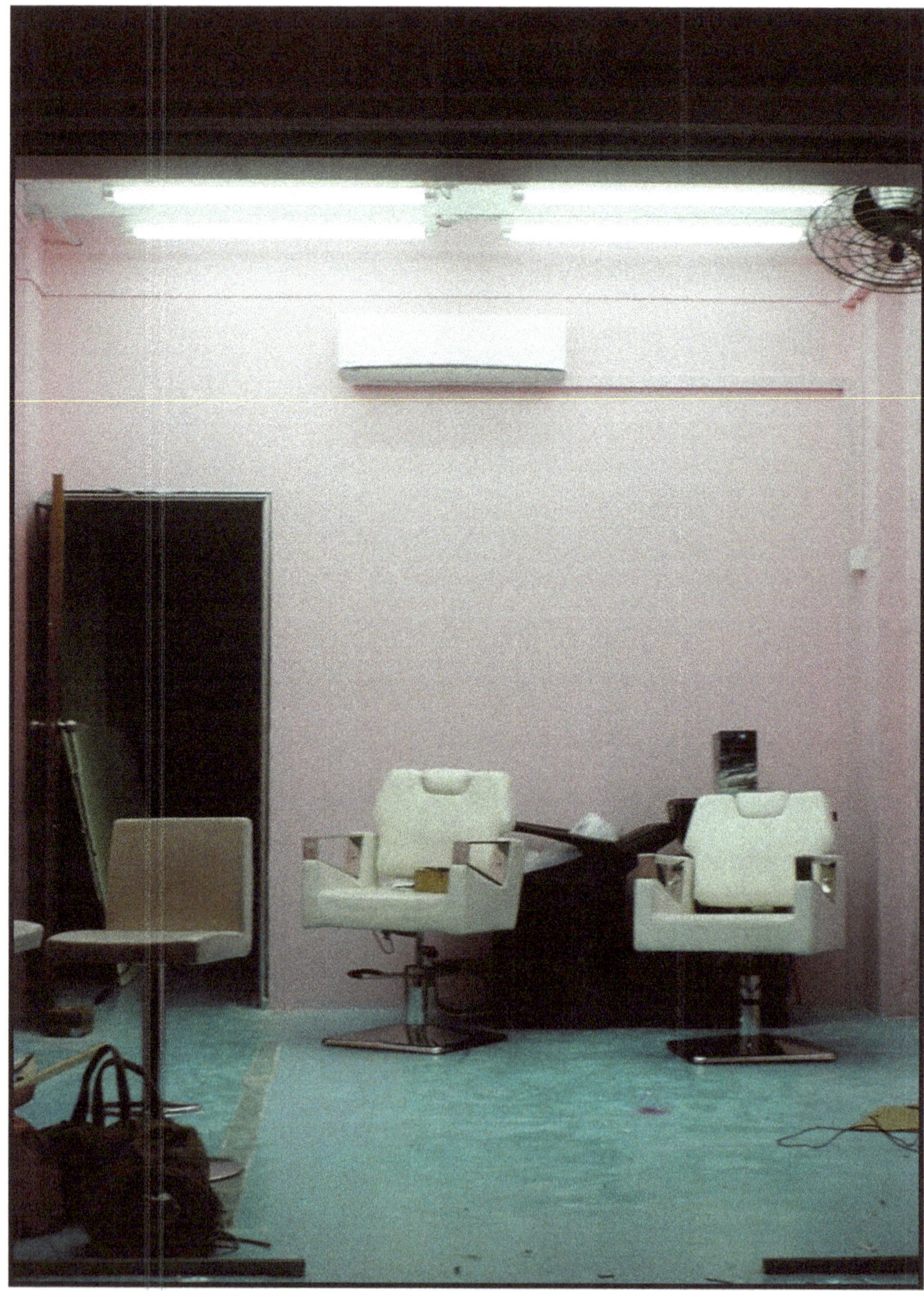

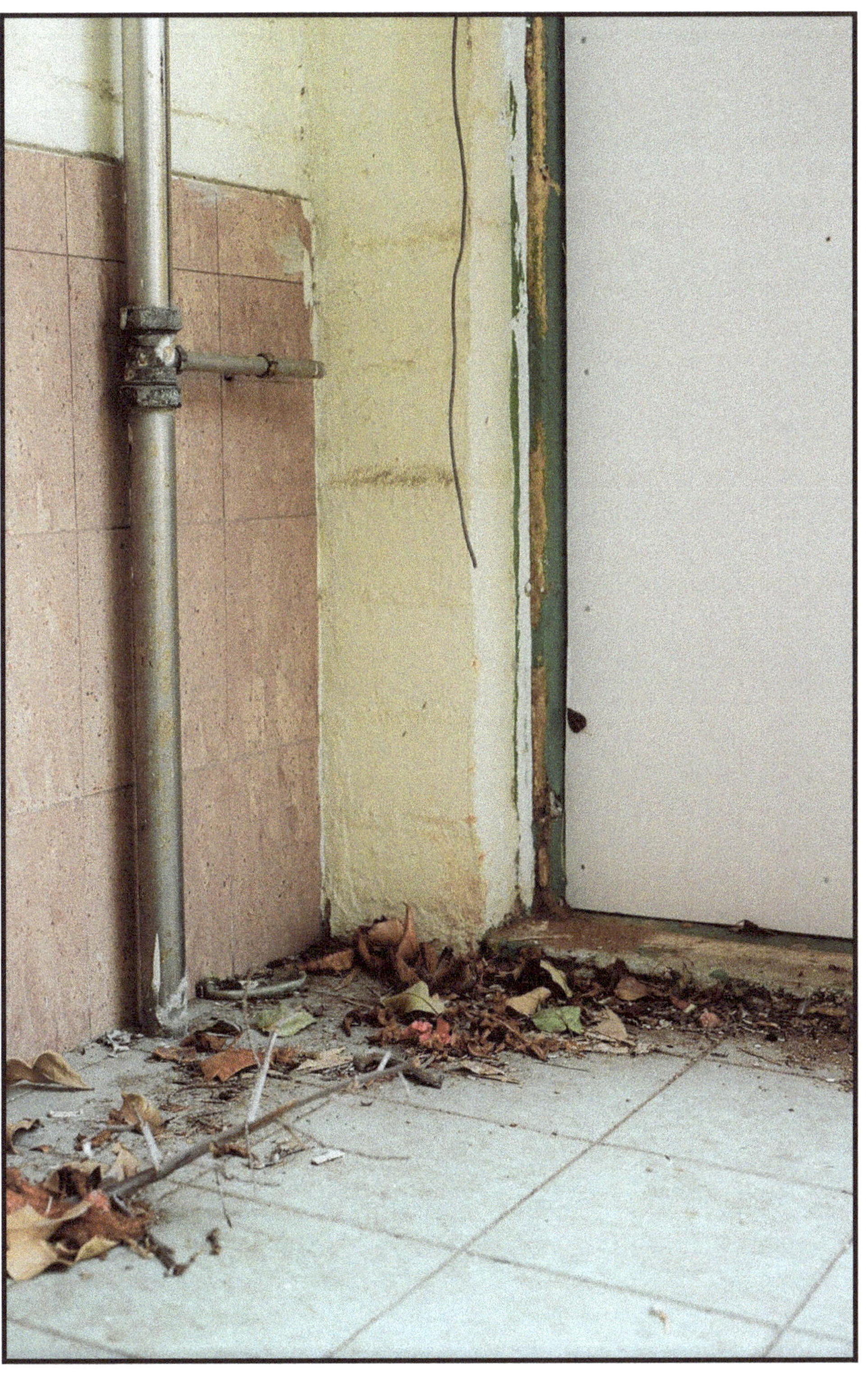

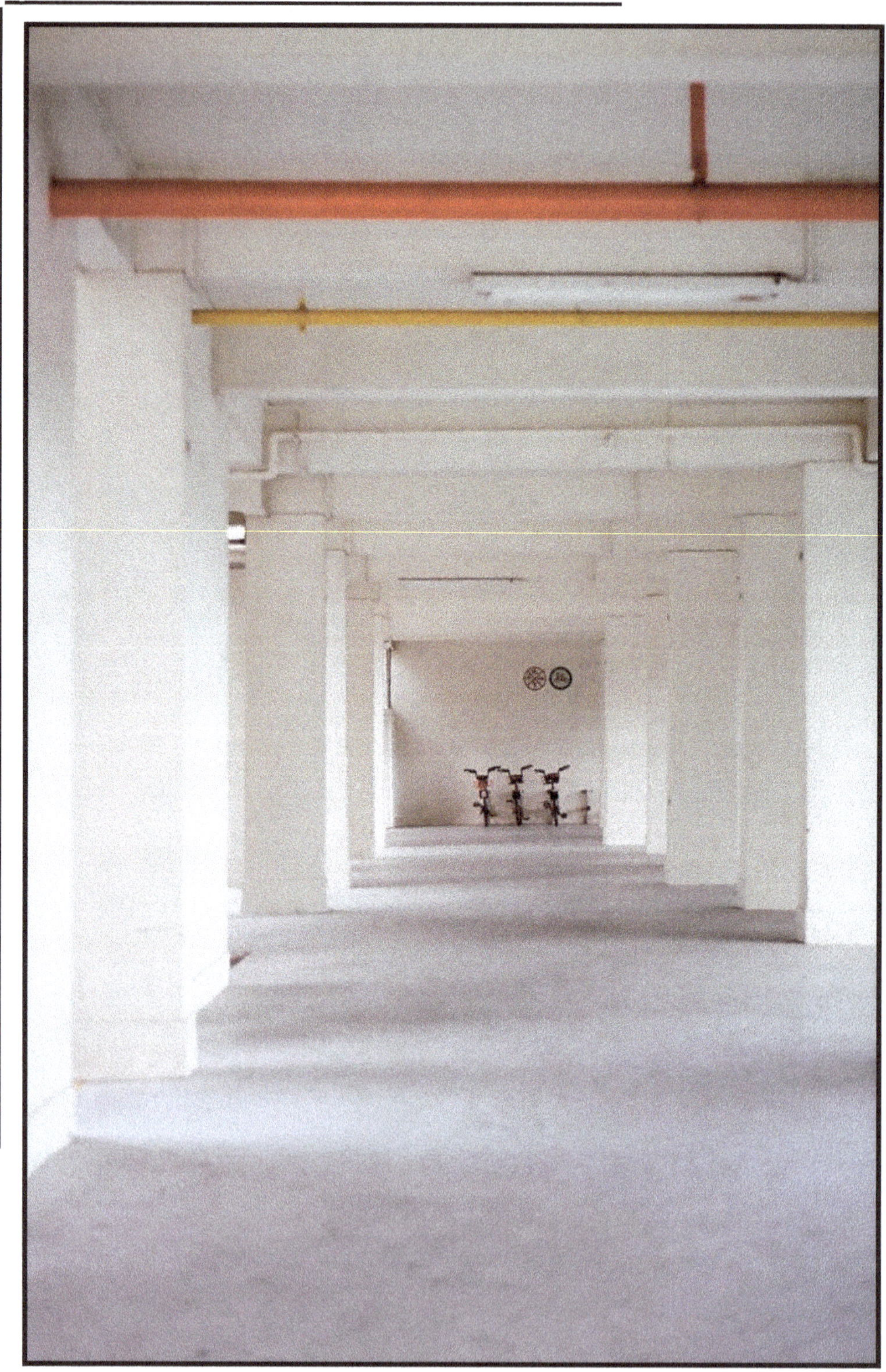

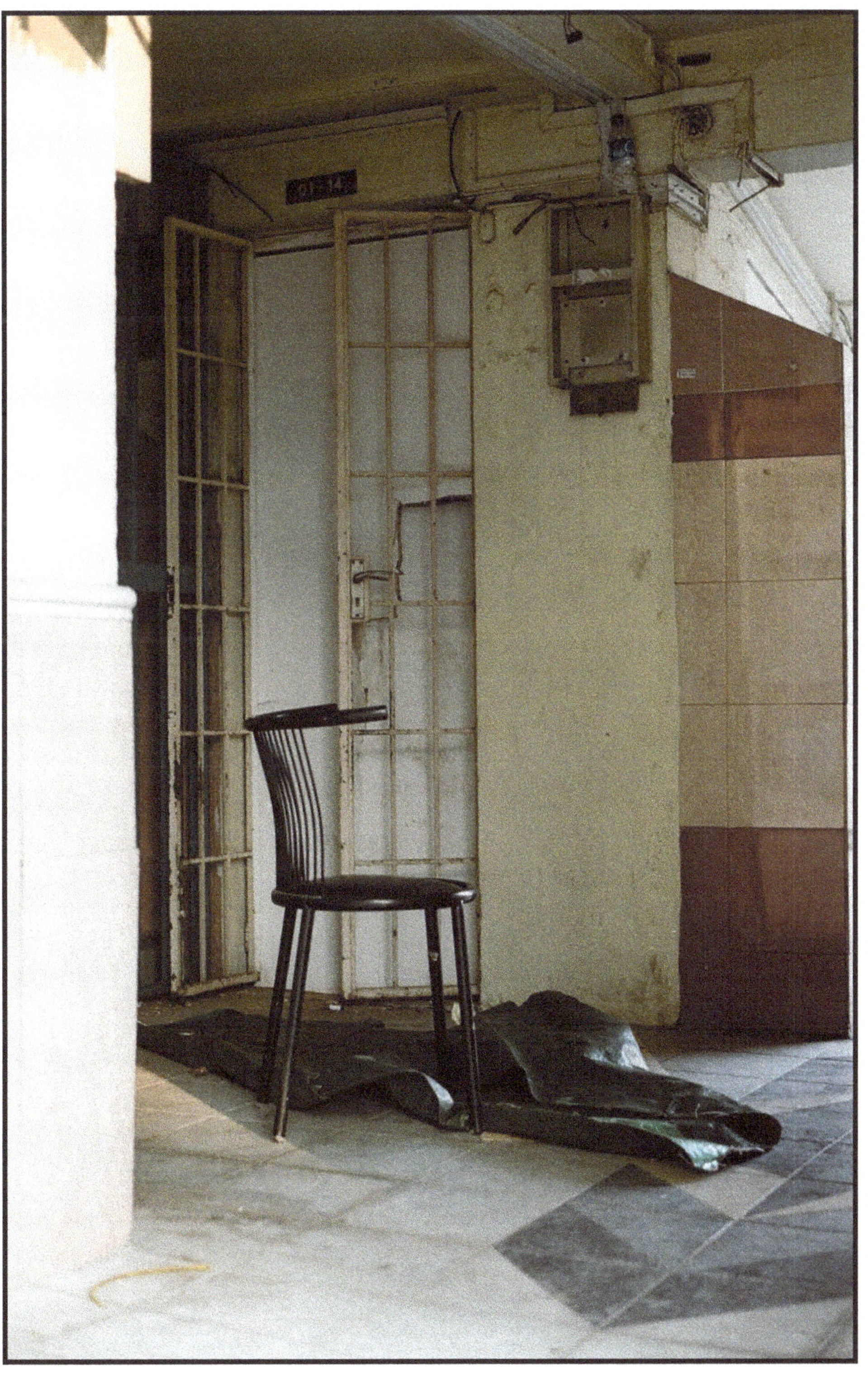

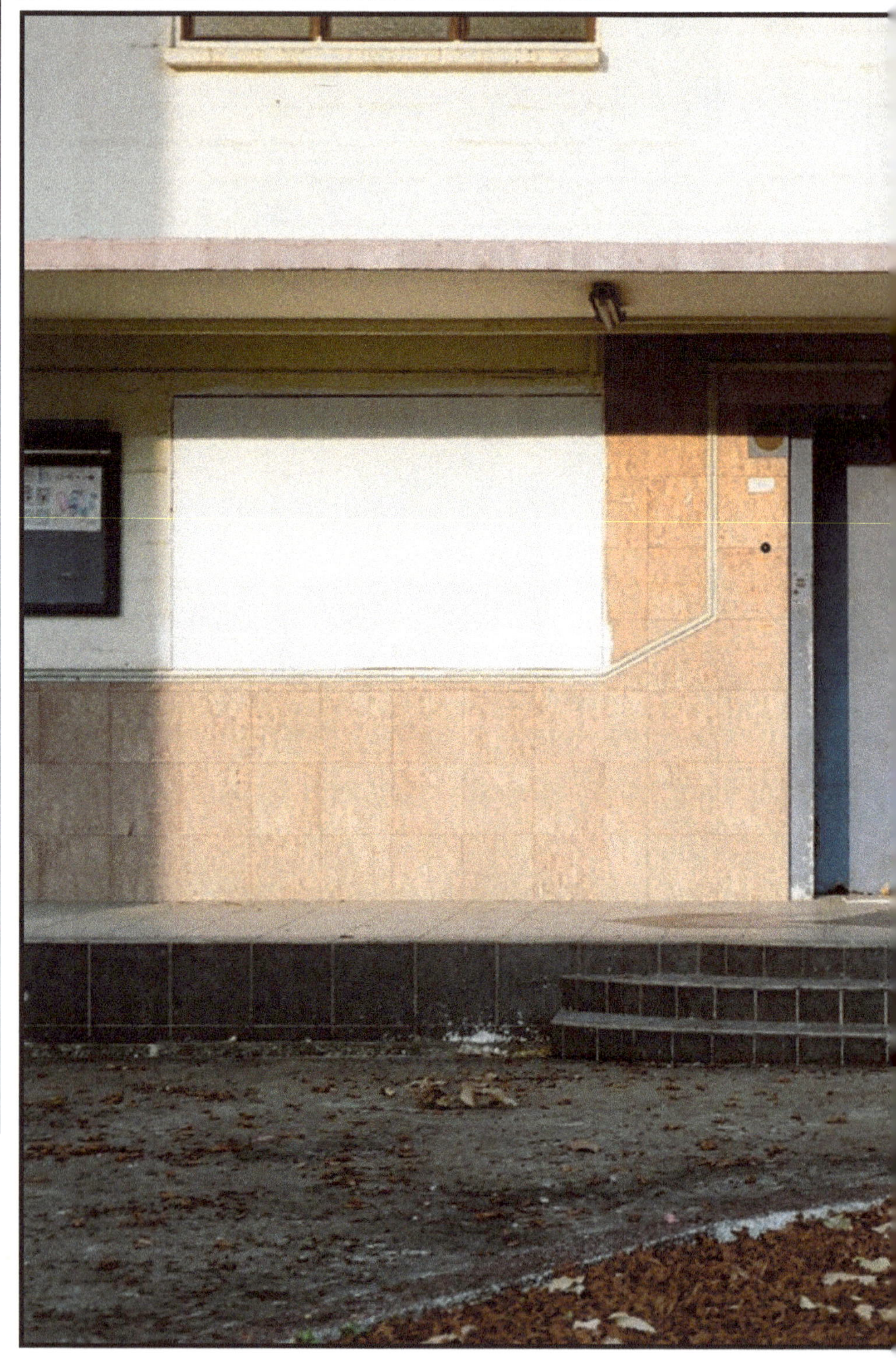

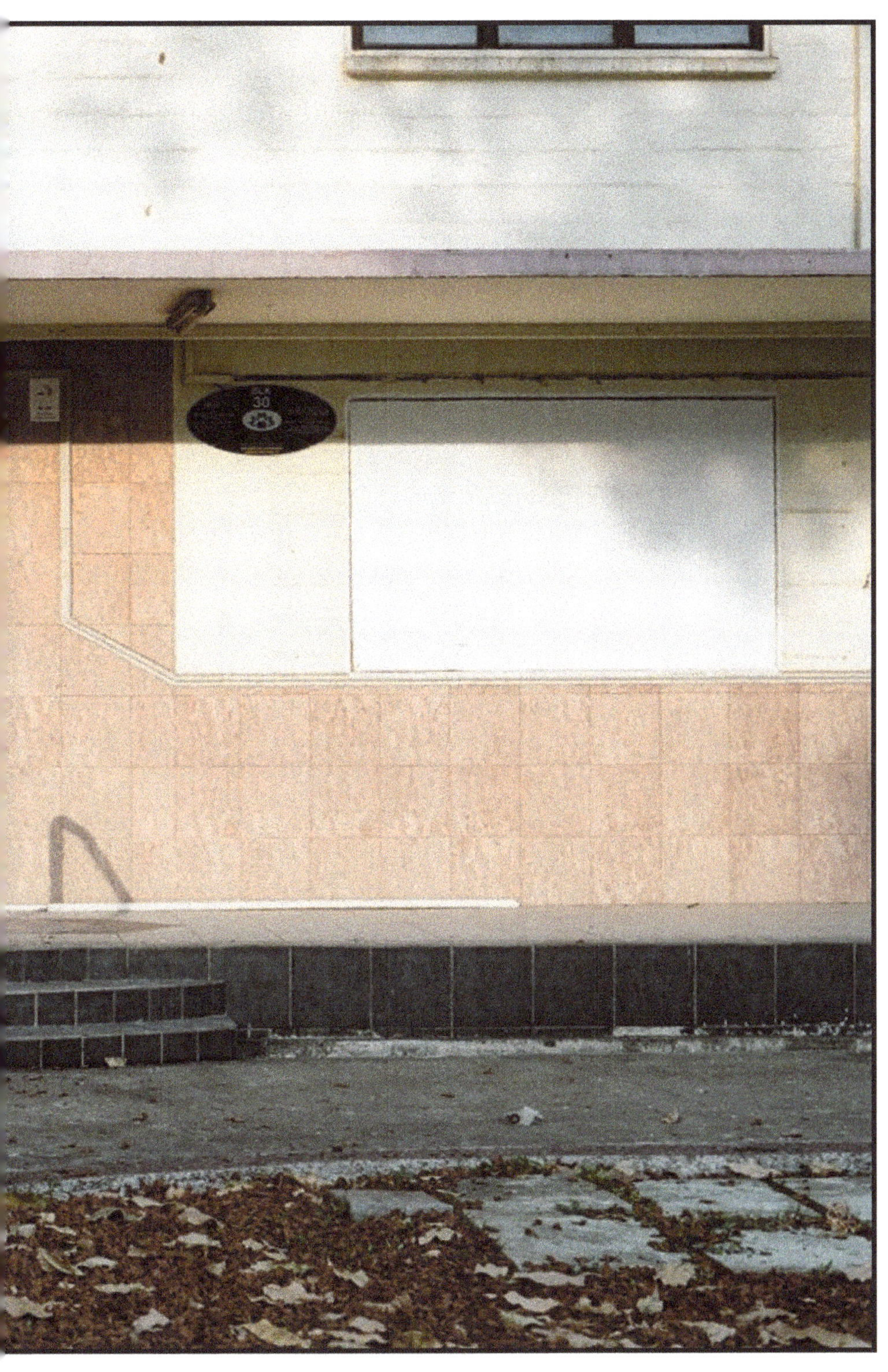

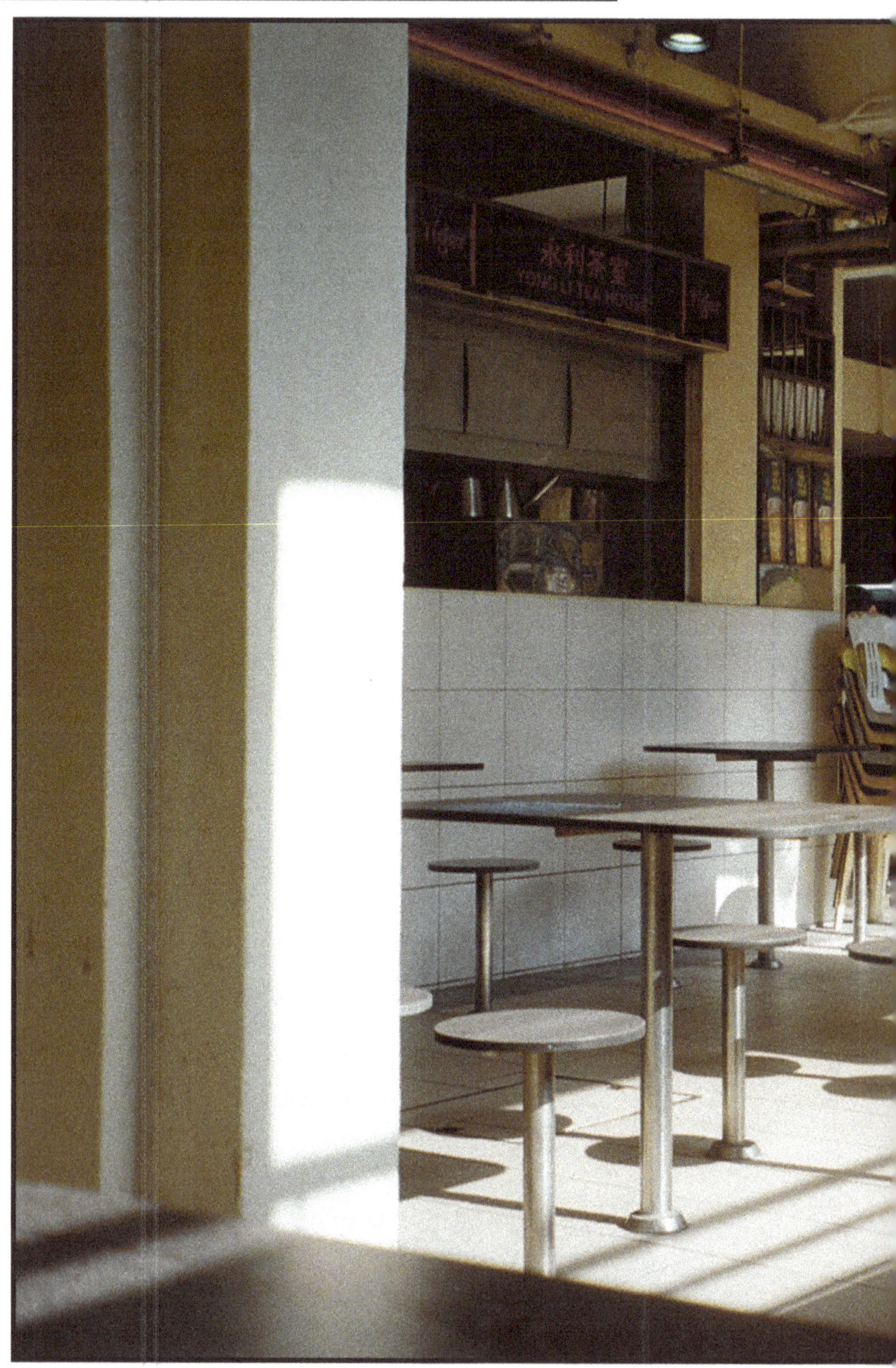

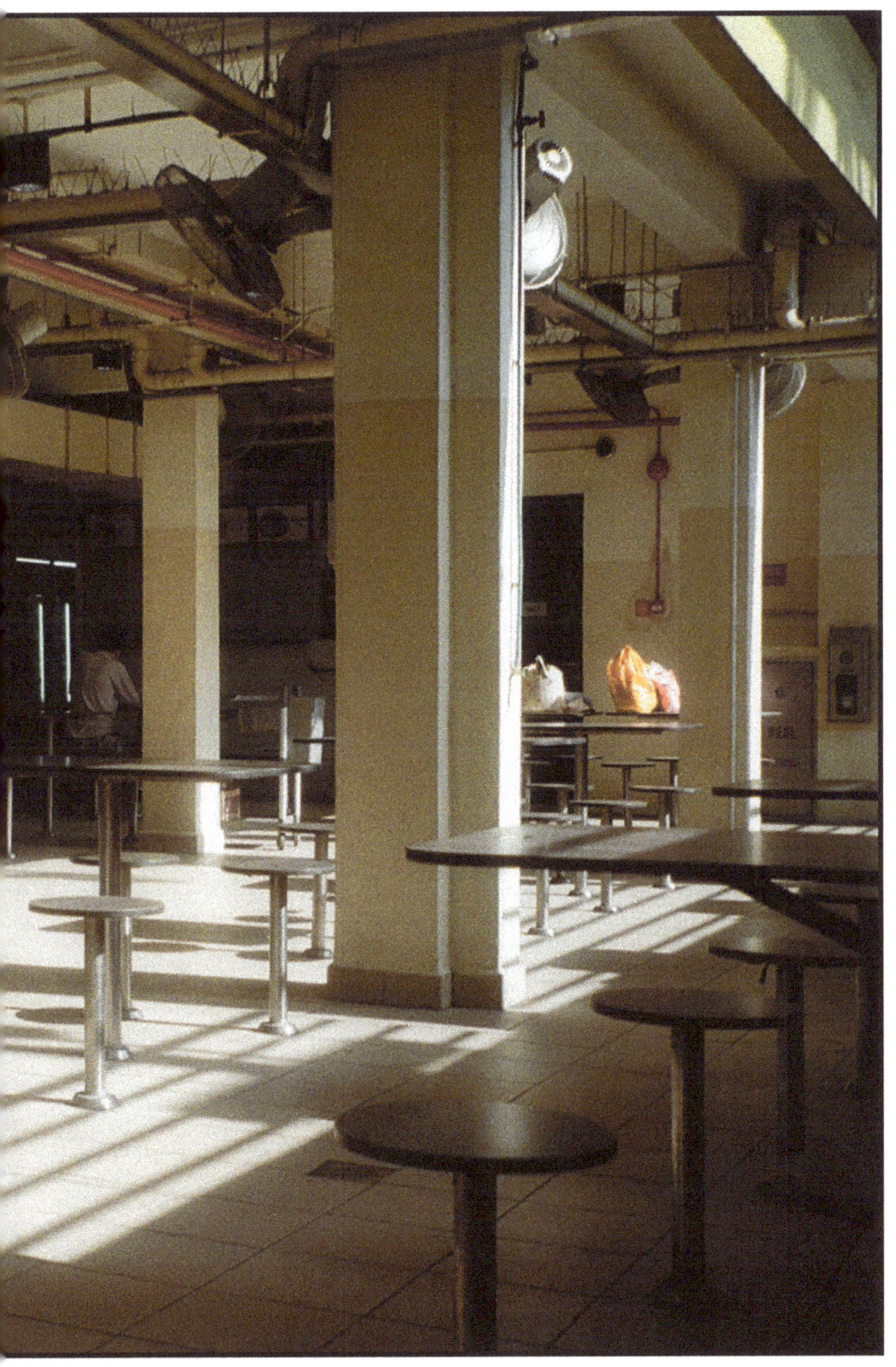

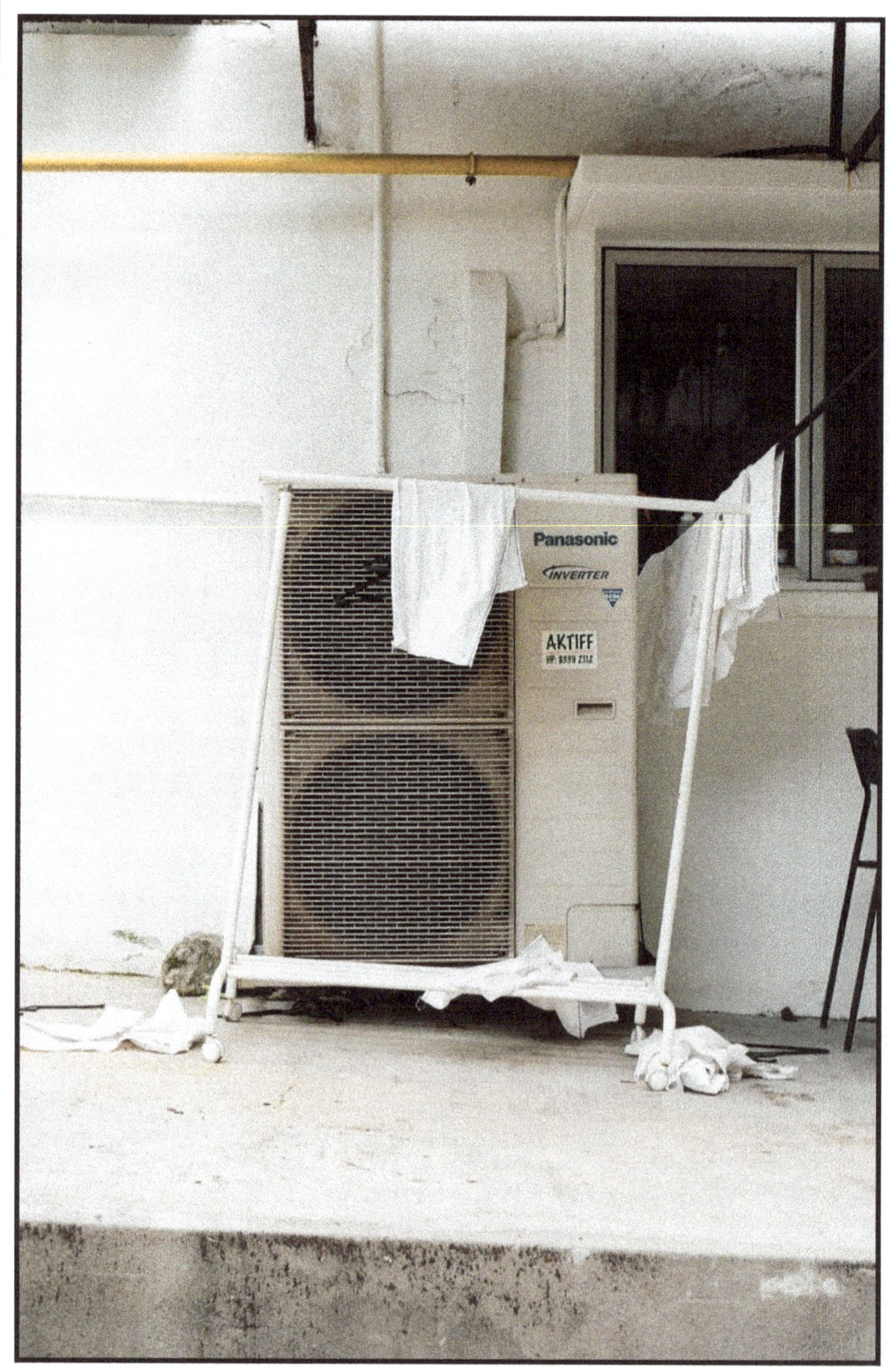

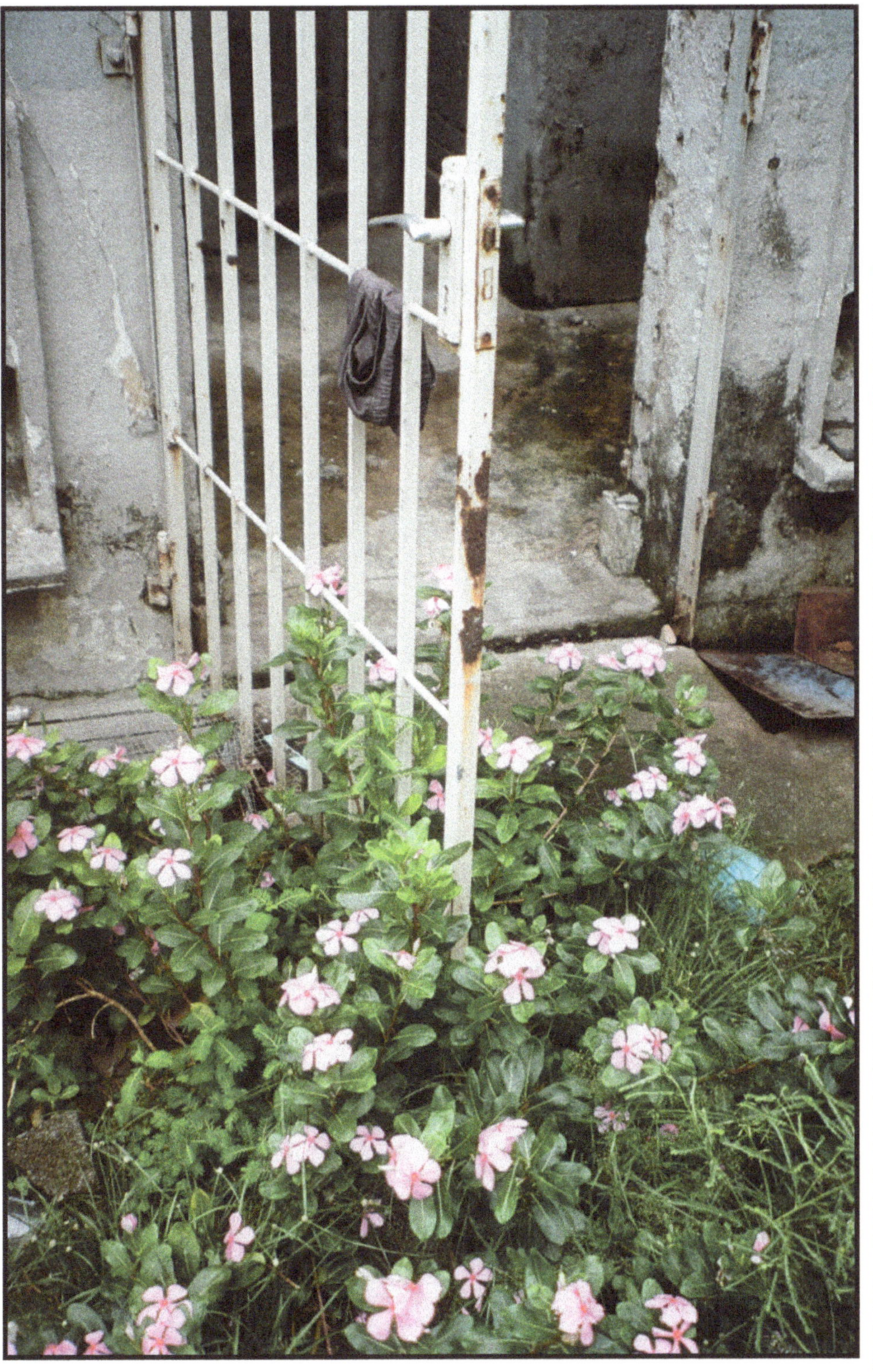

Dallas

Kryston Lopez

cold colossus
crane your neck
to the dingy wool of sky.
the trees collide:
       all verdant and crashing—

bright flash
-es of green
       -ness against

the oyster lid,
wet and murky.

it's almost brazen the way they

      bare

those shivering ornaments—
veins swollen with water
pulse with electric
chroma souls.

and the cars are beeping,
screeching
tires shriek homage to the
slick streets,
onyx sheets of asphalt
as they dodge
umbrella-huddled hunchbacks
that hopscotch
a   cr   o   s   s
puddled intersections.

pregnant sky,
Mother sky,
meets infant earth
with wailing city mouth
that drinks and drinks
her nectar.

Hallelujah
hallelujah
hallelu
-jah.

The Night After Our First Big Fight
Maegan Gonzales

In the dream, you are a sailor
and we marry the day we meet.

You have children and an ex-wife.
The children – ours, too – I see now vividly.

Our oldest daughter with hair long and black
since birth. Wild ringlets caught in the wind.
She cries with quiet green eyes, brooding.

Our youngest boy – still awkward in his body –
flails his arms and spins sand. You call to him
sandstorm, waves of yellowed hair swirling.

His eyes wide like coffee, ground, and dark ocean
marbled. He says *green is the strongest element.*

You are called to leave our family
for three months, maybe six – probably not
a whole year. I don't know how long
we've been married, but I live a lifetime.

There are days we return to this rocky beach
examining overturned sea stars
collecting sand dollars with our girls
stick-poking washed-up jellies with our boys.

Muddy, earth-tinted clouds churn the sky.
There are so many storms while you are home.
You know when they're coming – *an old salt's nose* –
and in the dream, you stay.

Radio Ocean

Valyntina Grenier

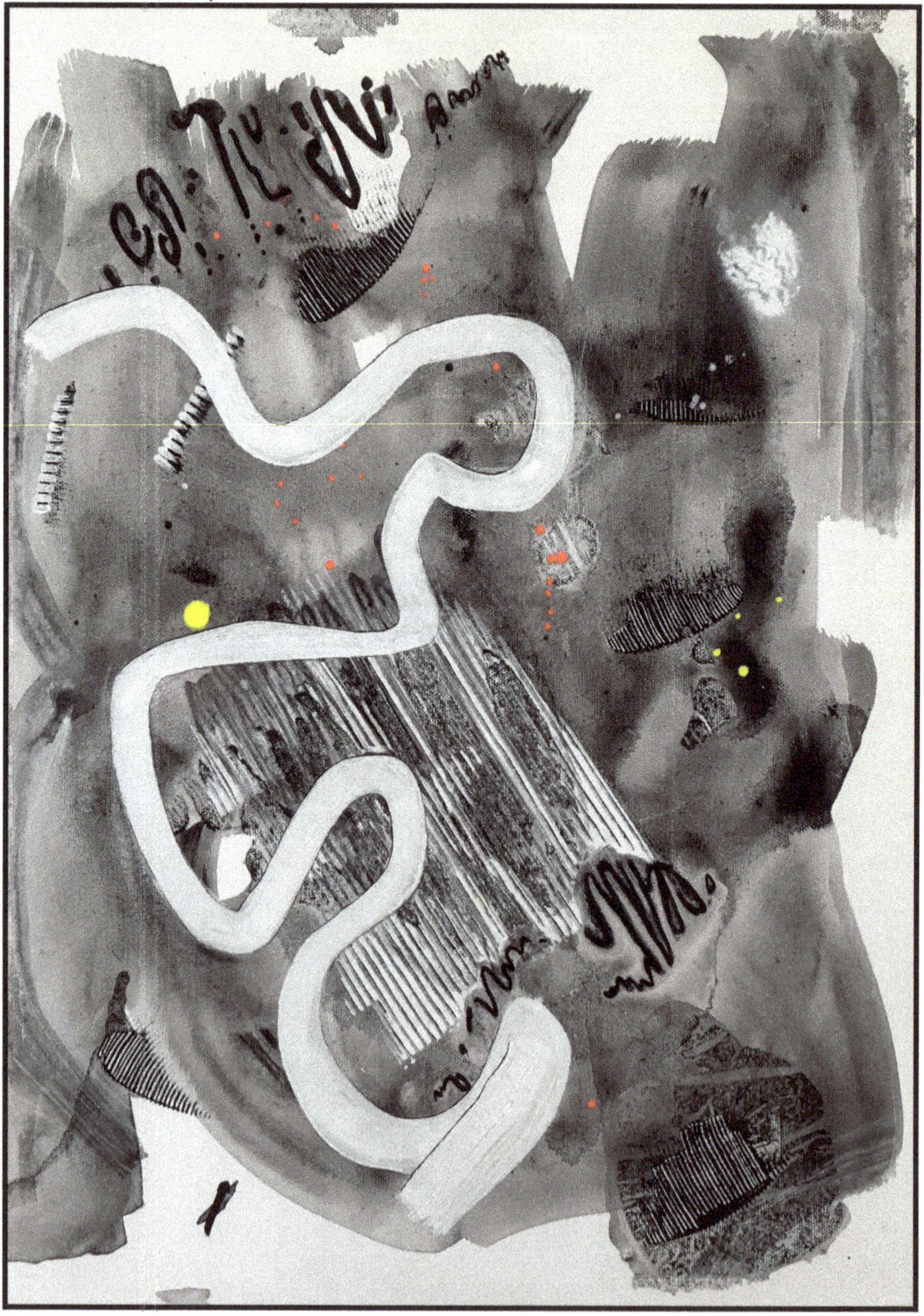

Bio Luminescent

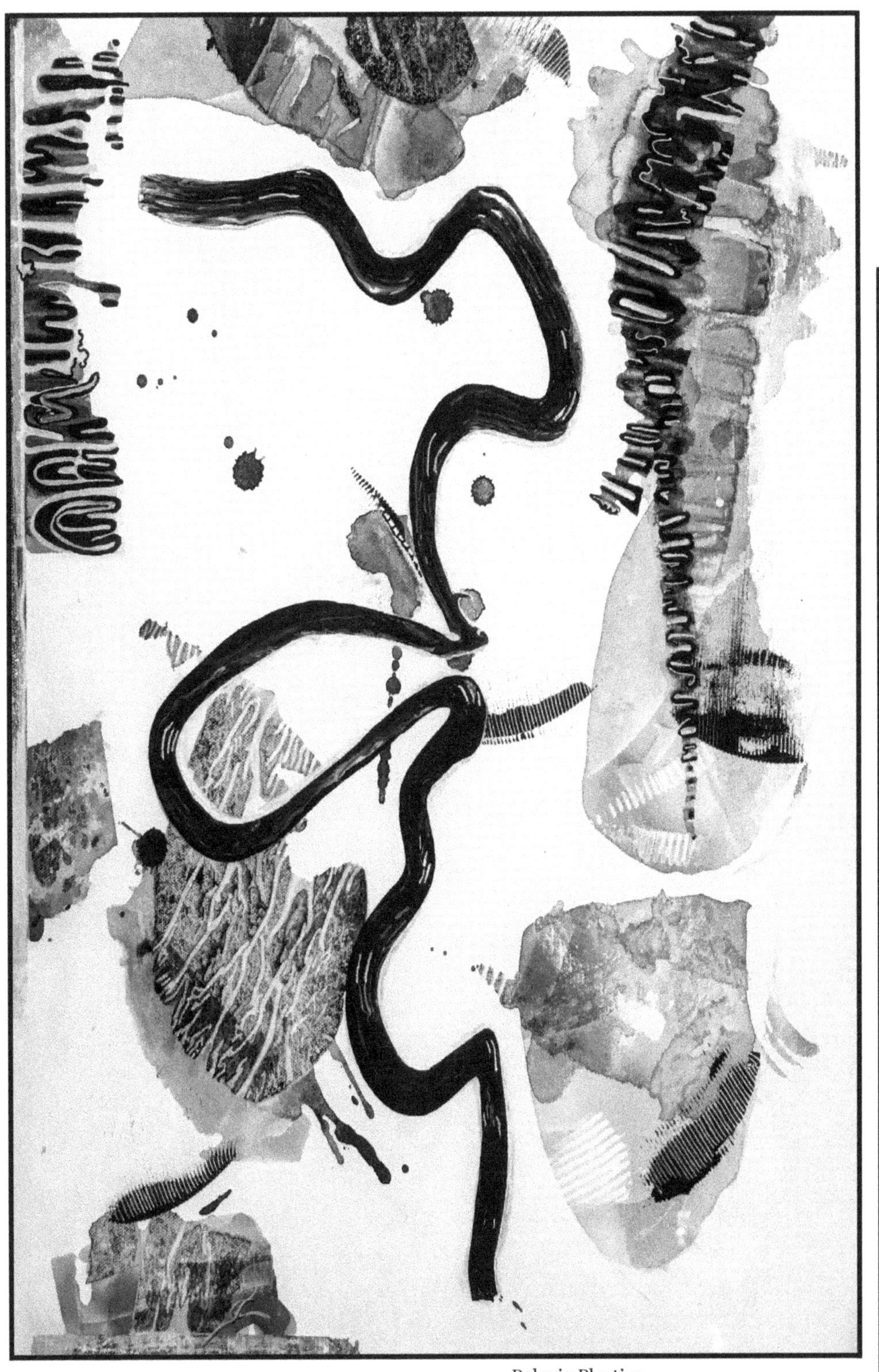

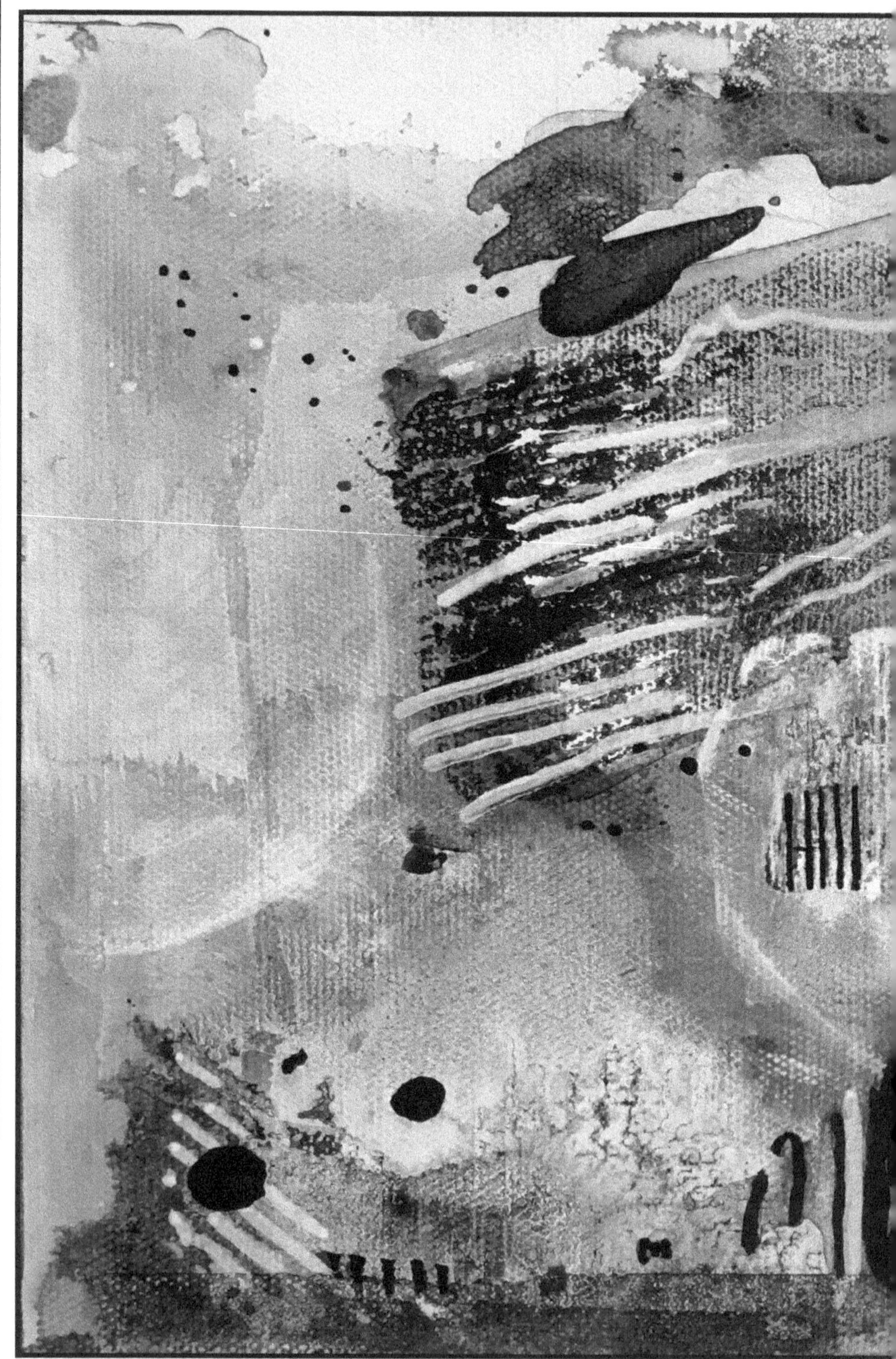

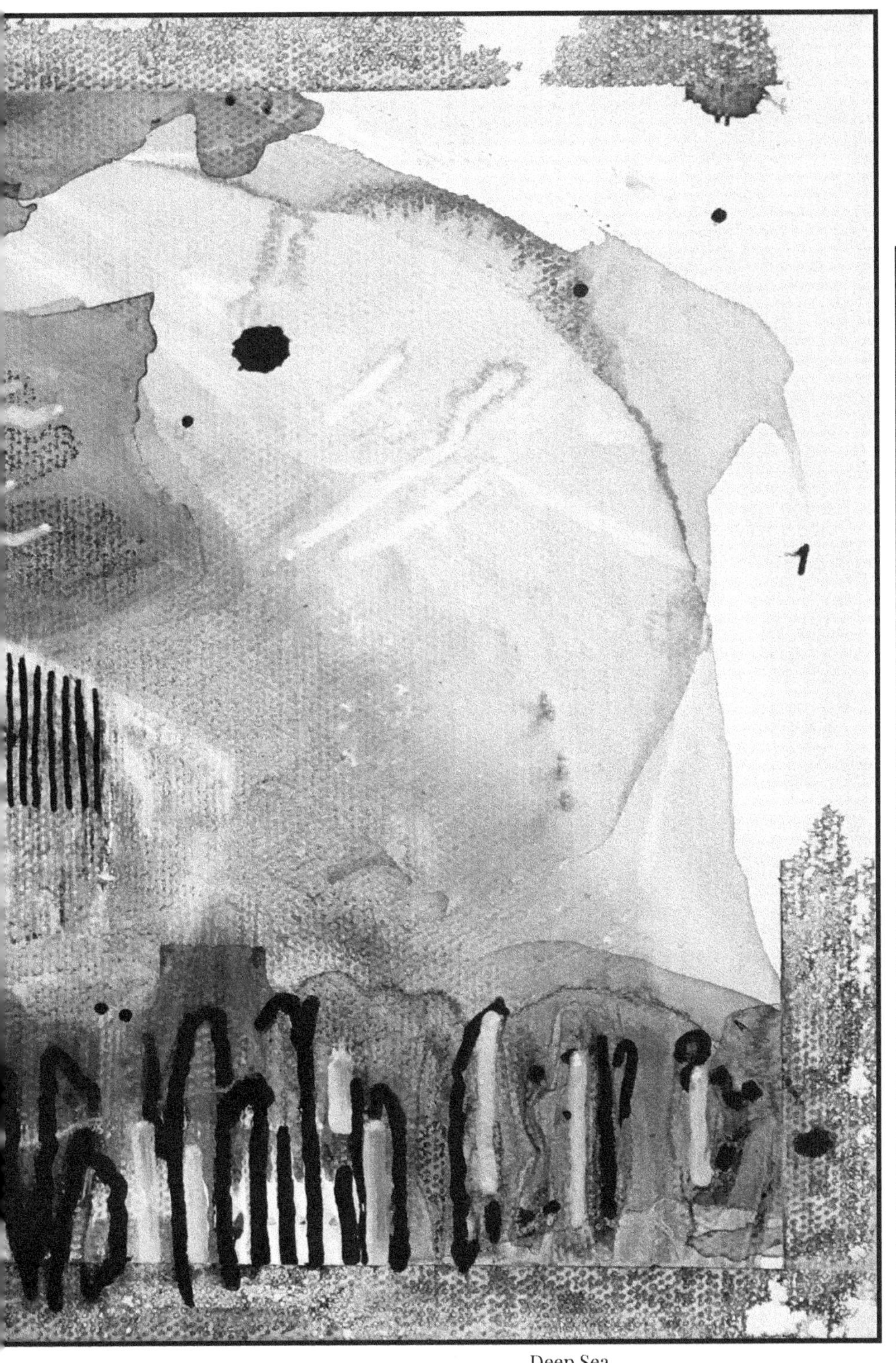

Deep Sea

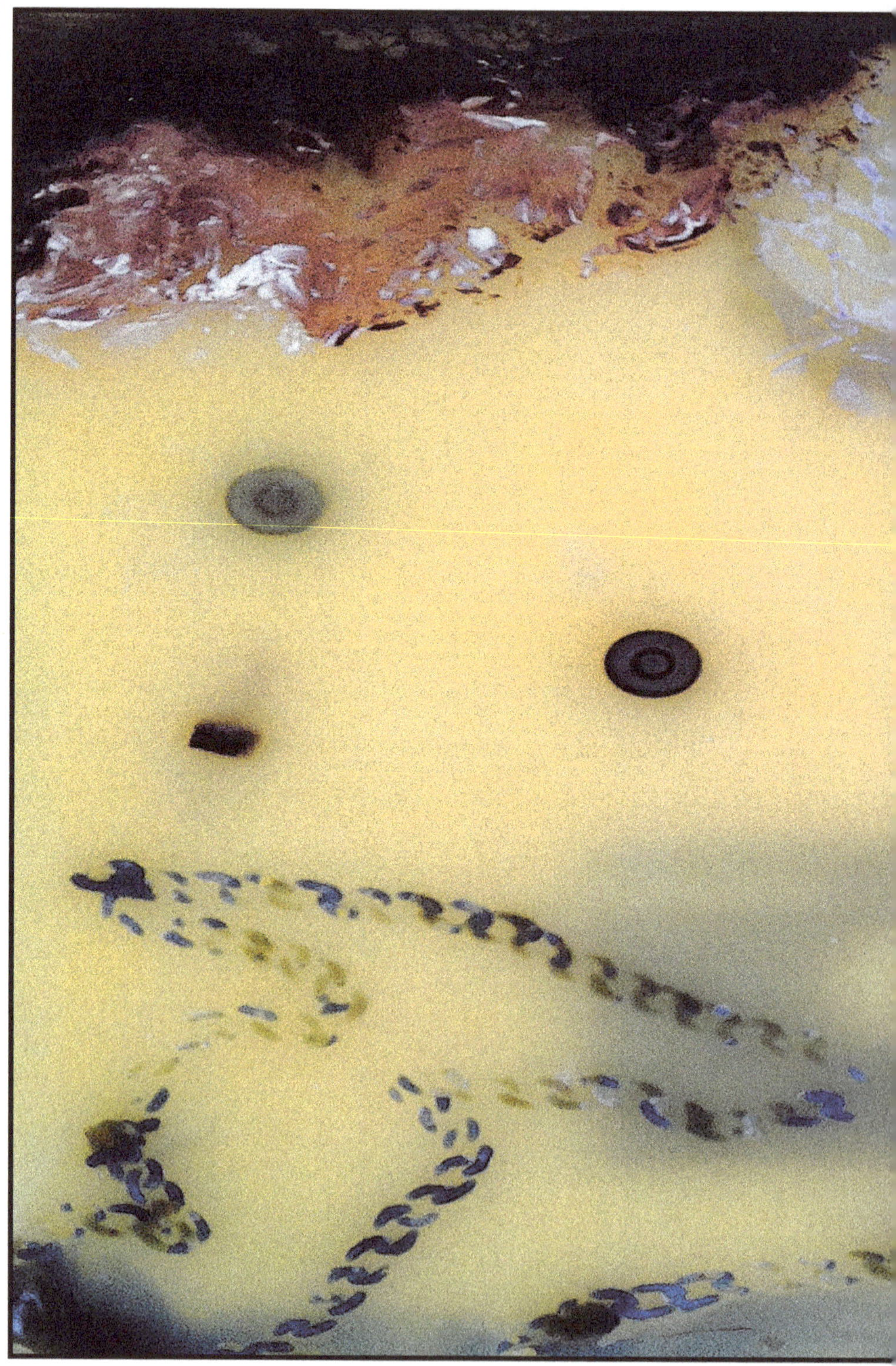

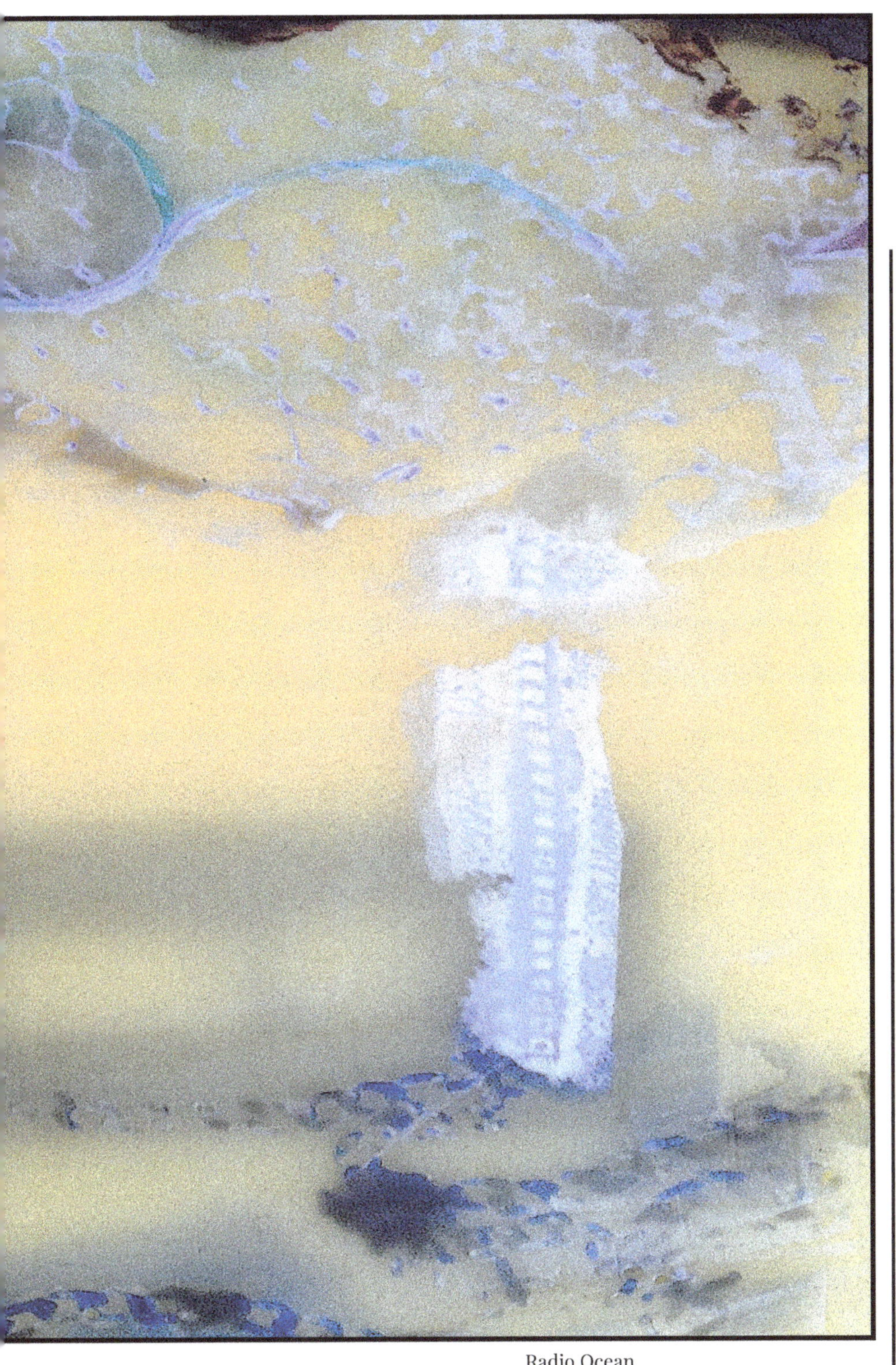

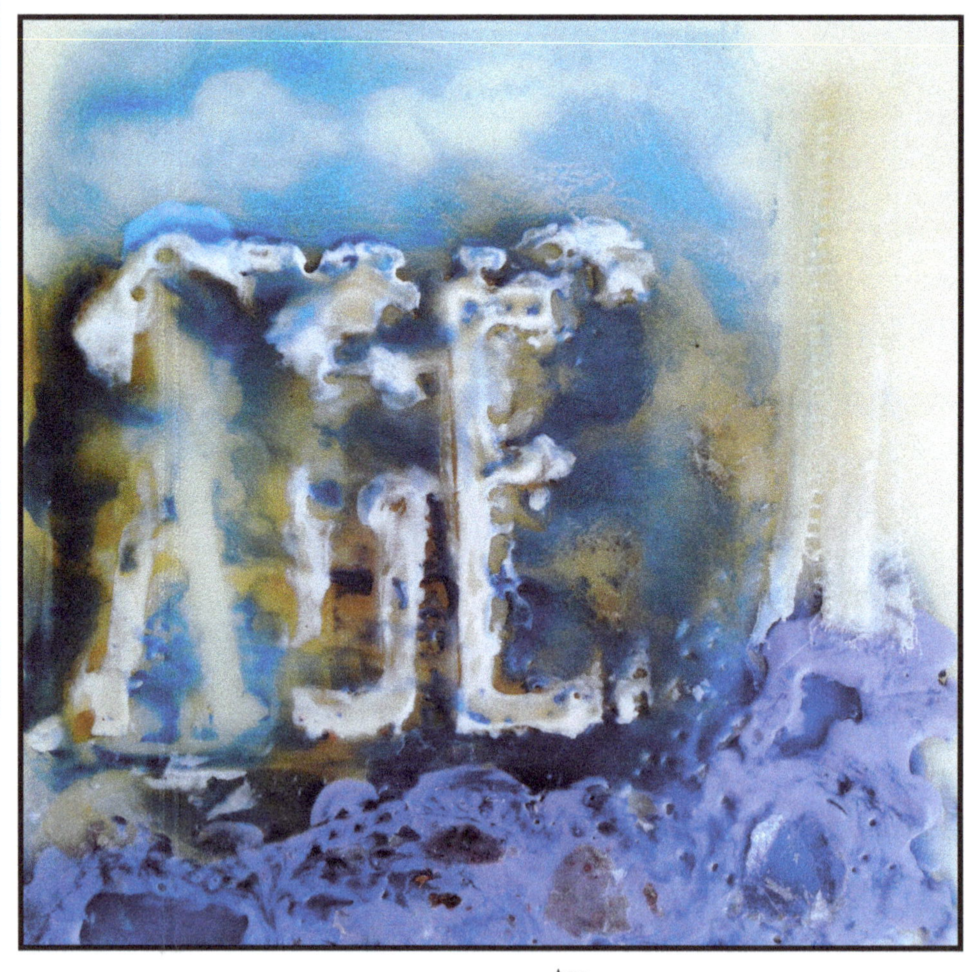

Age

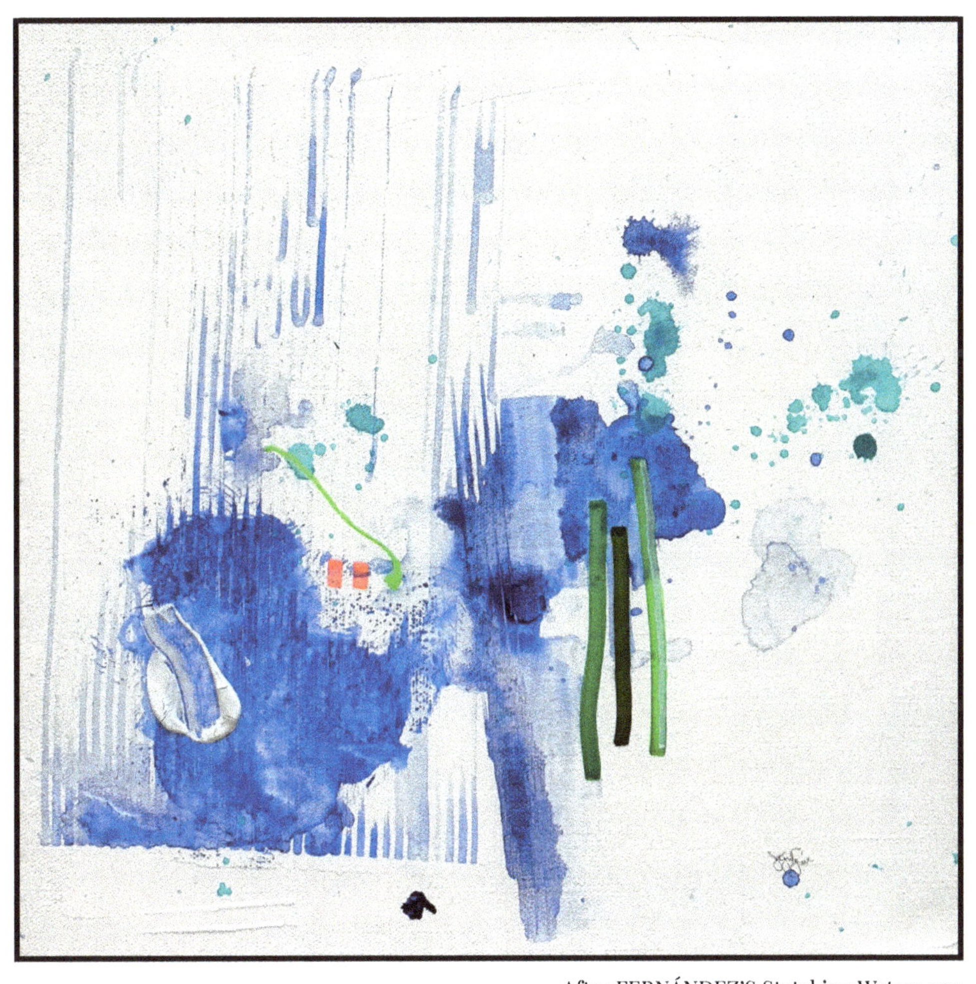

After FERNÁNDEZ'S Statcking Waters 350

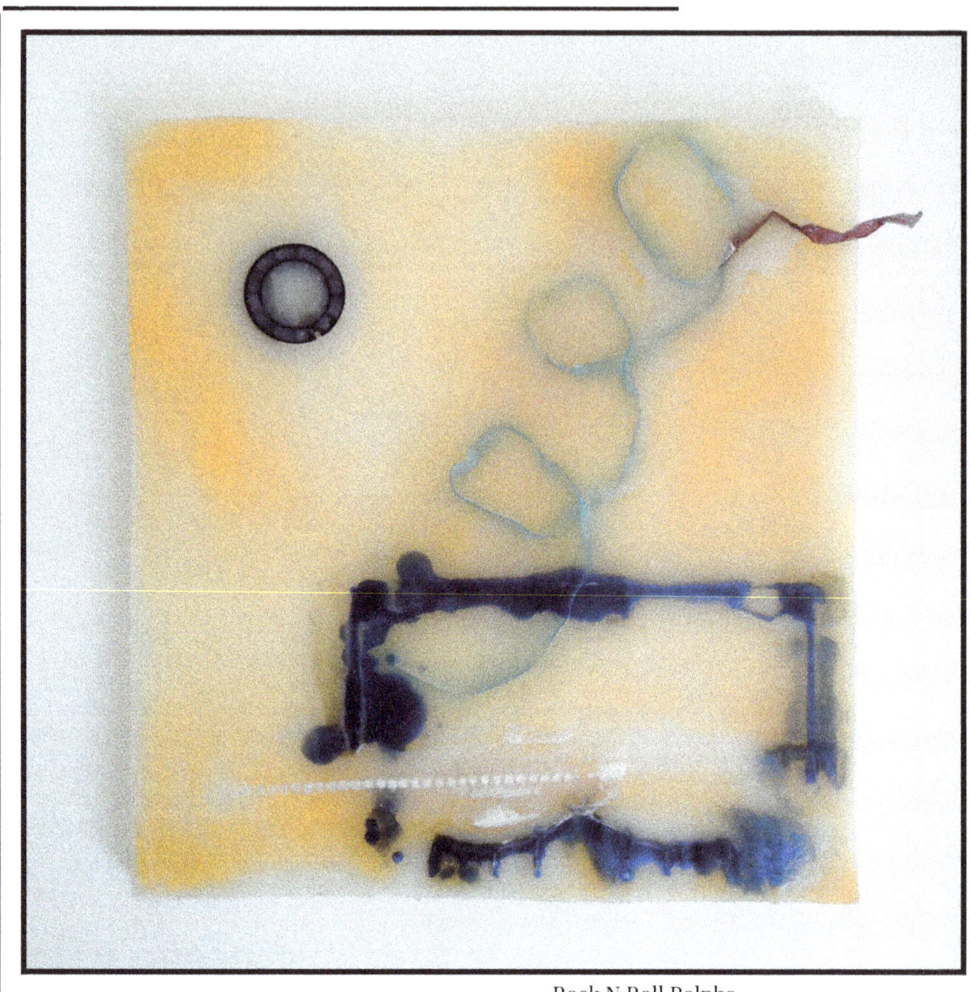

Rock N Roll Ralphs

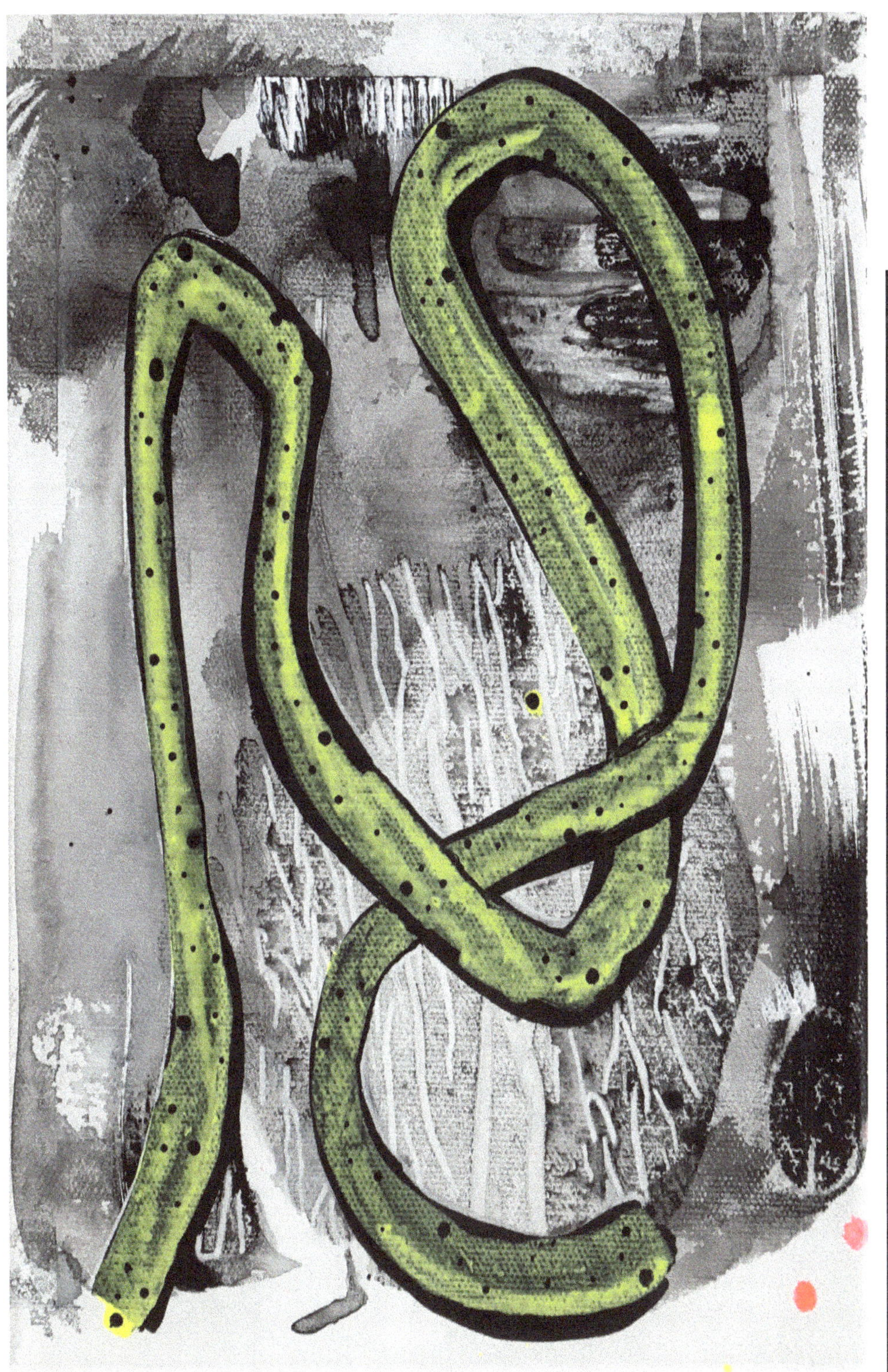

untitled

Patron of the Arts

Phoebe Millerwhite

We've been collecting art for years, my husband and I. It's different these days though, with the political climate such as it is. Now what we bring into our home needs to be more than just pretty, it needs to *mean* something. Example: my newest painting, just installed in the main living room, is a splendid piece by an emerging young artist. And what do you suppose the subject is? A maid! She's in a grey uniform and her face is obstructed so that she could be any woman. And she's vacuuming. It's inspired. The social commentary is astounding. Sometimes I just sit and stare at it. It goes without saying that I've never expected Lena, our housekeeper, to wear a uniform, that would be too Upper East Side circa 1985.

I've always felt very close to Lena, we've even let her come on vacation with us once or twice over the years. I would go so far as to say she's one of the family, practically, and I feel this new painting has brought us even closer together.

The artist capable of creating such a tour de force used to work in a warehouse, so he really understands what blue-collar employment means. Now he's making something of himself by representing, through his art, the kind of people he used to be. It also happens to be a great investment, the prices for his work have increased exponentially in just the last couple of years. And the museum shows! Too many to count.

I don't know if Lena has noticed the painting, although she has to clean around it so I suppose she must have. How proud she must be to work in a home where her employer would spend—well, I won't divulge how much, but a significant amount of money, six figures, for a piece of art venerating someone just like her.

These days all my friends are buying politically and socially conscious art. Art with a message, that's what we all feel connected to. One dear friend recently acquired a piece from Los Angeles; a huge mural painted on the side of a liquor store. Layer upon layer of graffiti on top of this old peeling stucco. If the owners had had their way, it would have been painted over because it was technically "vandalism." The neighborhood didn't appreciate it either, something to do with gang affiliations or some such. Luckily my friend saw it for what it was immediately: Art. Pure and simple. He had the whole wall removed, just sliced it right off the rest of the building like a mole and shipped it to his penthouse. It looks spectacular – the stark white walls and floor to ceiling windows contrasting with this gritty urban masterpiece. Stunning.

Speaking of recognizing art out of context, my husband brought home the most wonderful sculpture not long ago. Two worn leather shoes – they even had holes in the toes – which looked like they had been worn for years. Really authentic. The stories those shoes could tell. He bought them off a homeless man, although the man couldn't (or wouldn't?) understand what gems they were. Since it was snowing my husband offered to buy him some slippers from the nearby Duane Reade, on top of the more than generous $20 he gave him for the shoes themselves. My husband is very conscientious – frostbite is no fun. The shoes look simply darling on a custom-made pedestal positioned just so in our foyer.

It may be a cliché, but life sometimes does imitate art, even becomes art. Not long after purchasing the painting of the maid, I walked into the living room and what do I see? Lena, right in front of the painting, vacuuming. Imagine! So meta. It would never even *occur* to me to ask her to wear anything other than her usual jeans and a t-shirt, however the idea of seeing her in a matching grey uniform going about her tasks with her immutable counterpart in the background, honestly it gives me chills. I would never ask her... well, perhaps one day, just for fun...

Women Today

Christine Friedman

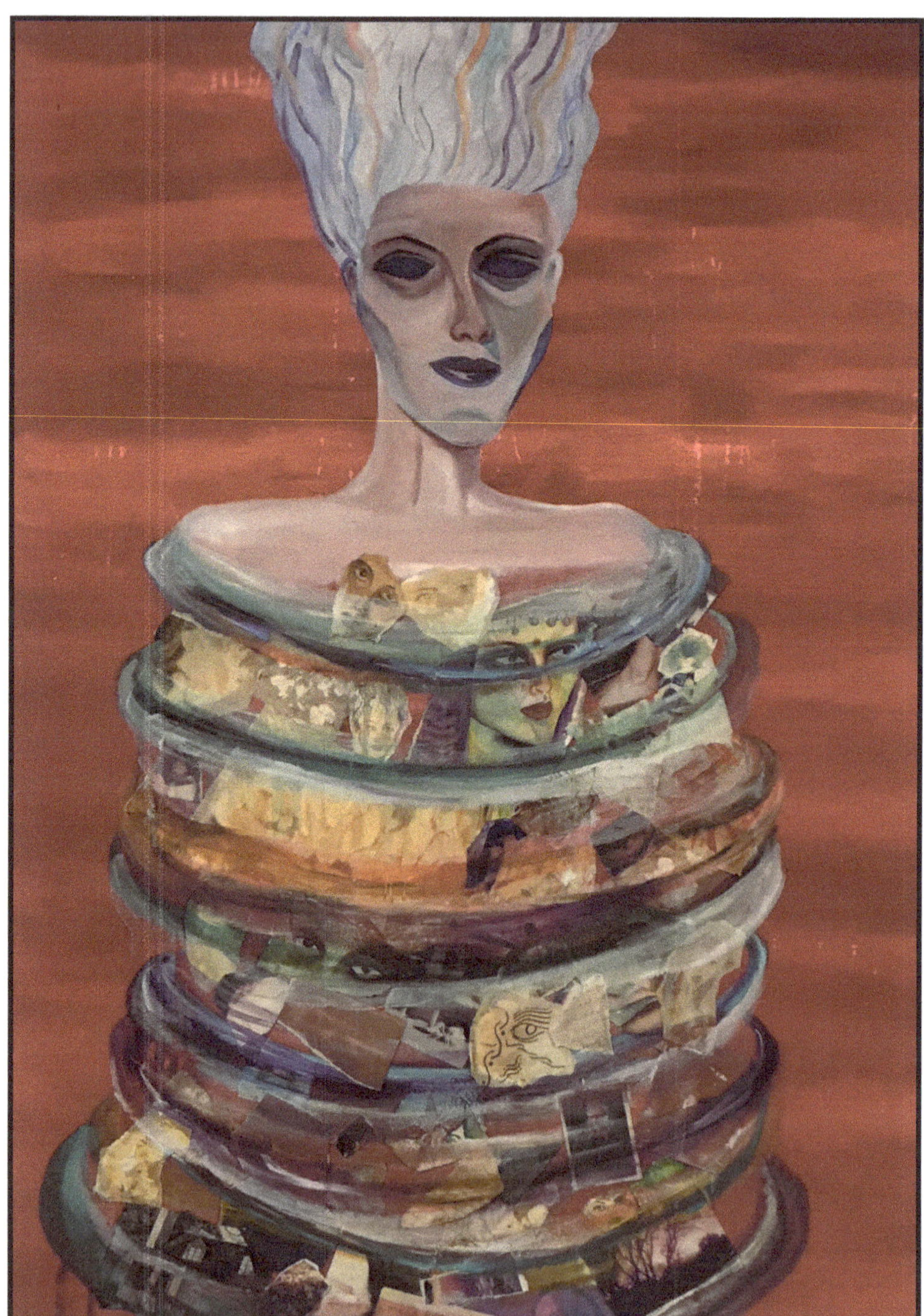

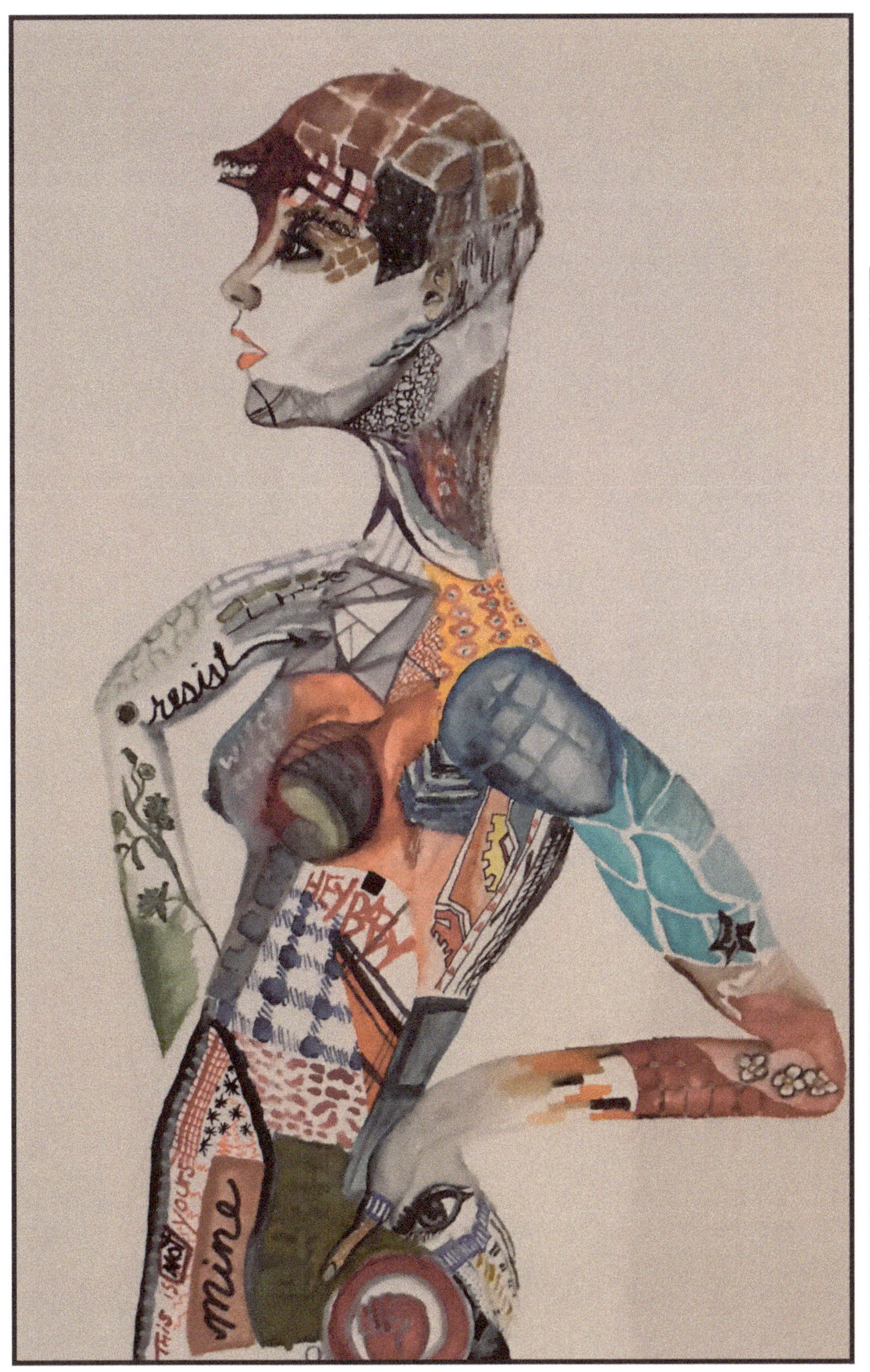
resist
HEY BABY
mine
THIS IS NOT YOURS

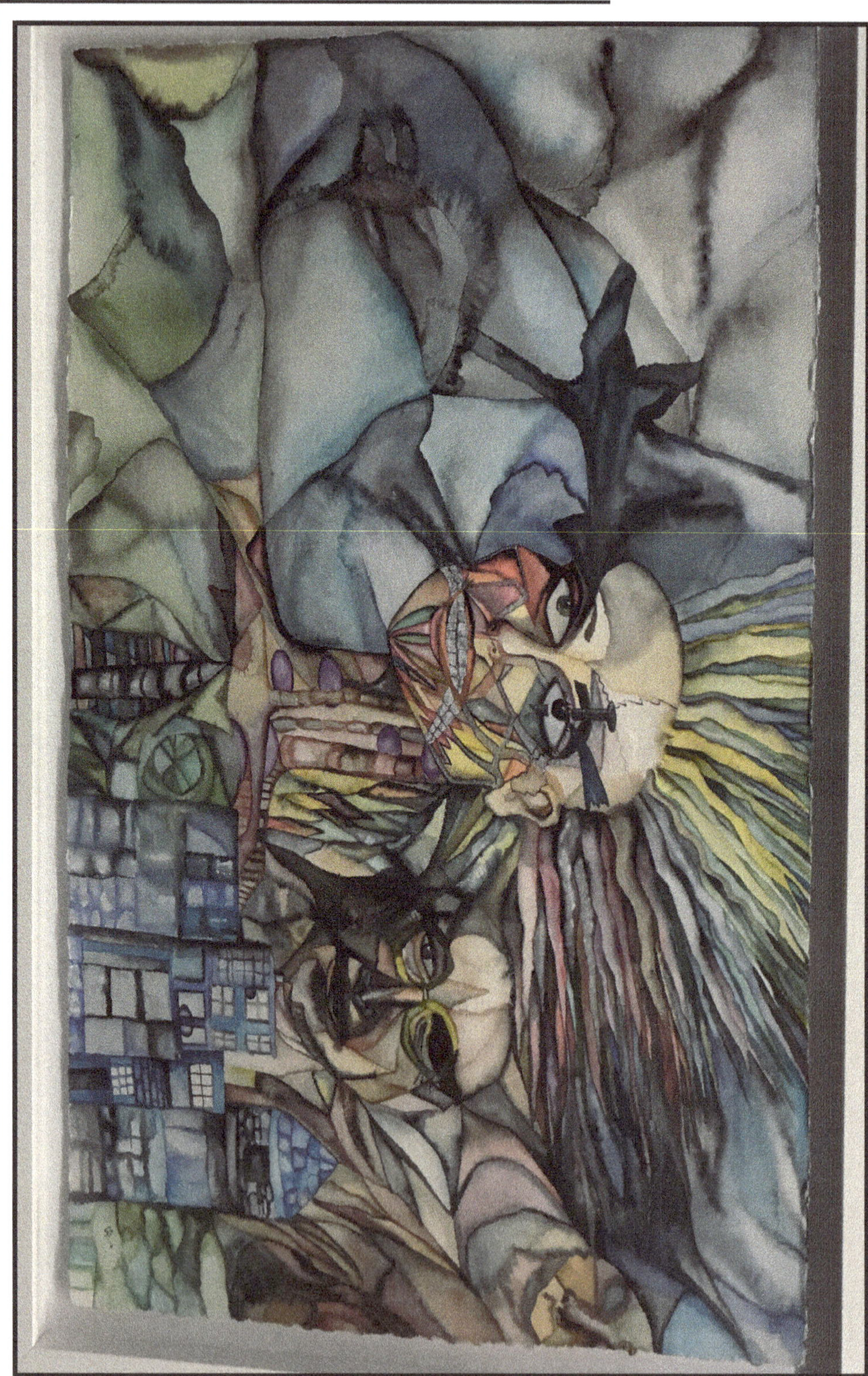

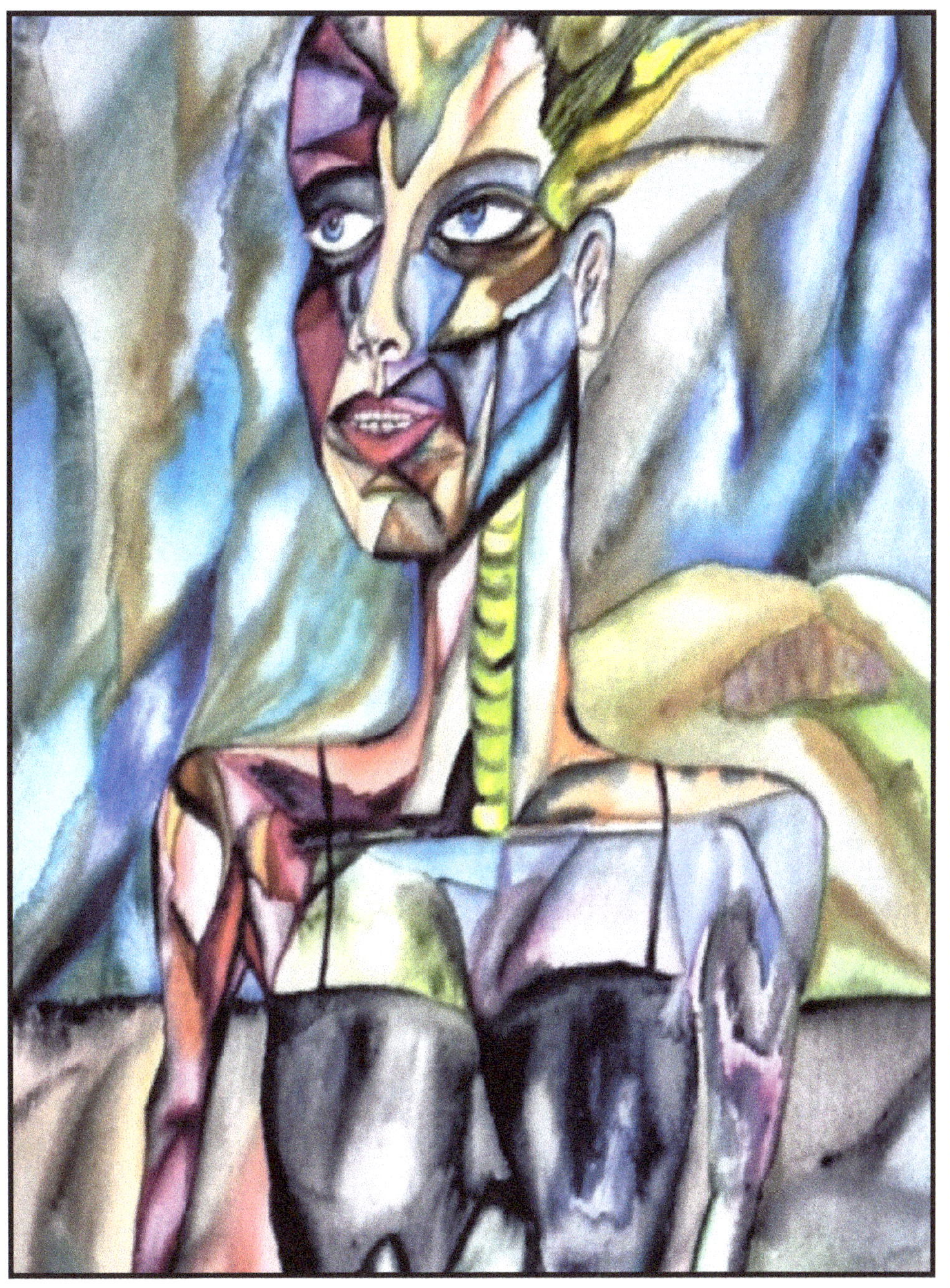

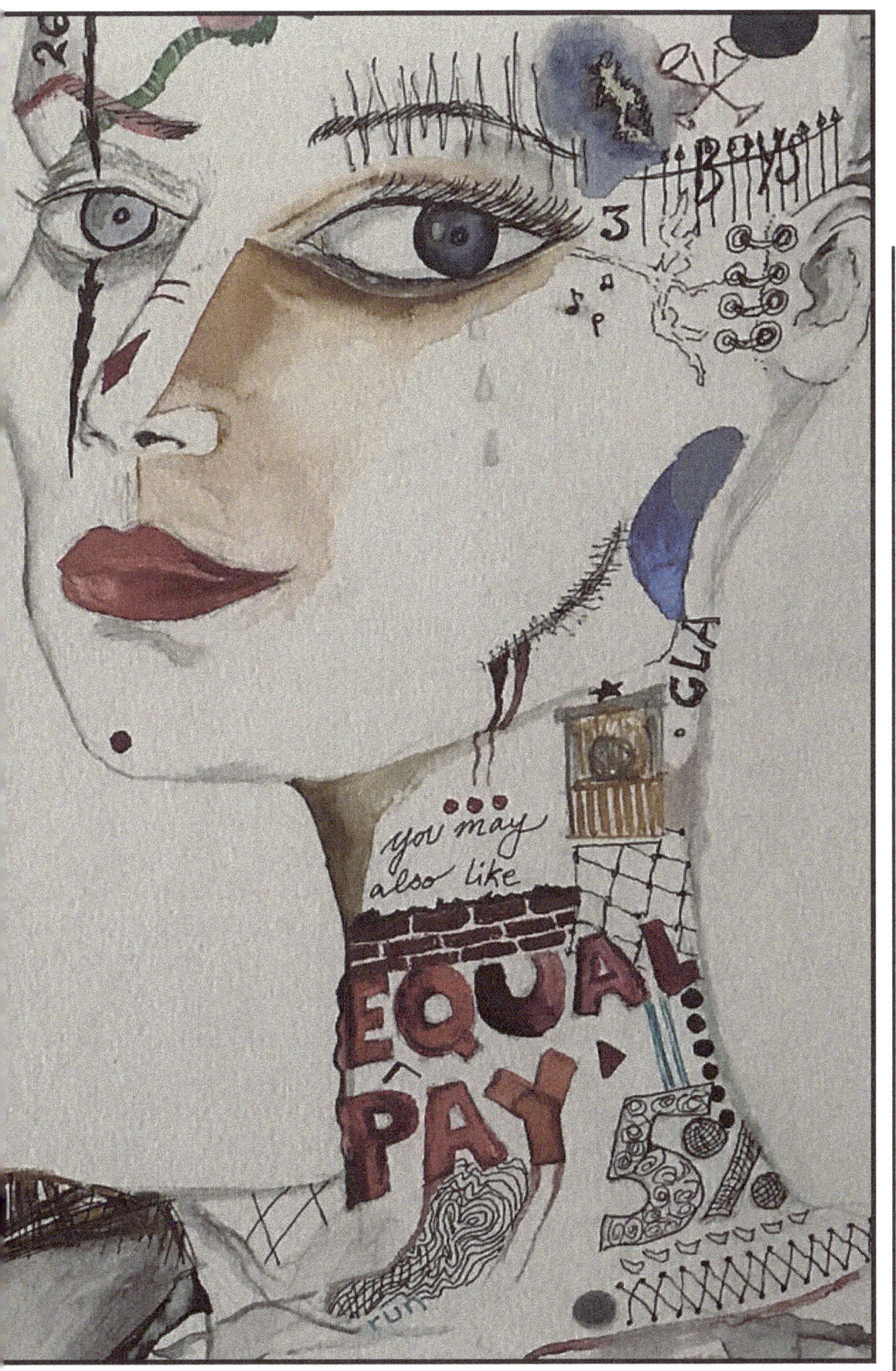
BOYS
you may
also like
EQUAL
PAY
5%

Long Distance

Stacey Walker

Your postmark is a blue bruise
from Germany. It is smeared—
the letters blur and bleed together.
I wait hours Tuesday for your
secret dog-eared message. The smell
of smoke and pub alcohol—your dark
ale hair and hangdog slouch.

Friday is Amsterdam--
your daybreak home, and soon
one from Belgium. I stack
them, to the left
on my desk
study how their right
corners all bend where you
sign your name.

Not all are even, some
are crooked and severe. I touch them
and see the cardstock fibers ripple—
how they fold in on each other, tiny layers
of paper—tiny layers of you.

Remember a month ago,
our Sunday in Eindhoven.

Now, I rub the ink. There
is a measure
of pressure in the lines of each
letter, a small thumb print
in ink, your left hand smears
greeting my fingers
back-and-forth—I rub
memorize your *Love*.

I want your permanence
and the long slender bridge of that *L*
to tangle me to you, hook me
with its bottom lip. I want that
from you, but next week
you'll be speaking Dutch,

falling out of love—
falling out of me.

SOMEBODY GET ME AN URN ALREADY

Samantha Madway

Speech bubble never said *love*—
notes never written, never read.
So good at Simon Says: rigged the game
to convince myself it's better to bet against,
no suspense:
                 blush so big it turned full body.

No offense, but, means something bad
is about to happen. Better to let it rest.
Better still to plead no contest.

I volunteer to be entombed. Seal the exits
myself, get lost in a windowless room.
Destiny is doom, waits to pounce where
fact meets fate, asphyxiate me, then
blame self-hate:
                 fuck pearly gates.

The devil is an about-face.
I don't believe in saving grace.

Circles and Beads

Natasha Moskaljov

We forget. So

we cut our bangs again,
find the same people

to love again,
break time apart

losing the same
pieces to start again.

I forget. So

I wish to pass you
on the busiest street

in town, walking
runway model steps,

talking English
on the phone.

You forget. So

you step aside,
my back unknown

graffiti on the wall
that you erased.

Time forgets. So

it ticks from twelve
and back again

as I count my days
before I fall.

Perhaps you do too.

Life is just a bead in
the prayer of the world.

"Sharecropping"
Cindy Sams

You on your knees, whiskey on your breath,
the moon a tangerine slice in the pre-dawn sky.

Light waves from my side-porch beacon back-lit
your hair, the ink-black strands swaying and stretching
through my fingers like a dark flag about to unfurl.

Sharecropper, you called me, because I rented my
Tiny red shack on the lake, while you were on loan from
the Big House next door. A tenant farmer and the landed

lord: our crop a yield of uneven proportions tilled in the
dark, on the sly, complicit with the nearby fish and waterfowl
that flipped and flapped as quietly as they knew how.

Our work after hours went uninterrupted, the seamless sowing
and reaping at the water's edge impeded only by circumstance
and the perils of time.

Who says the illicit won't grow well at night?
Here, a cluster of Moon Flowers, second cousin to the Morning Glory.
There, a pair of Four O'Clocks whose bright petals opened at the close
of day, then sealed themselves shut as the sun awoke.

An annual without promise of harvest, and you with no acreage
to spare.

Conquering Instant Gratification Project

Barrie Stark

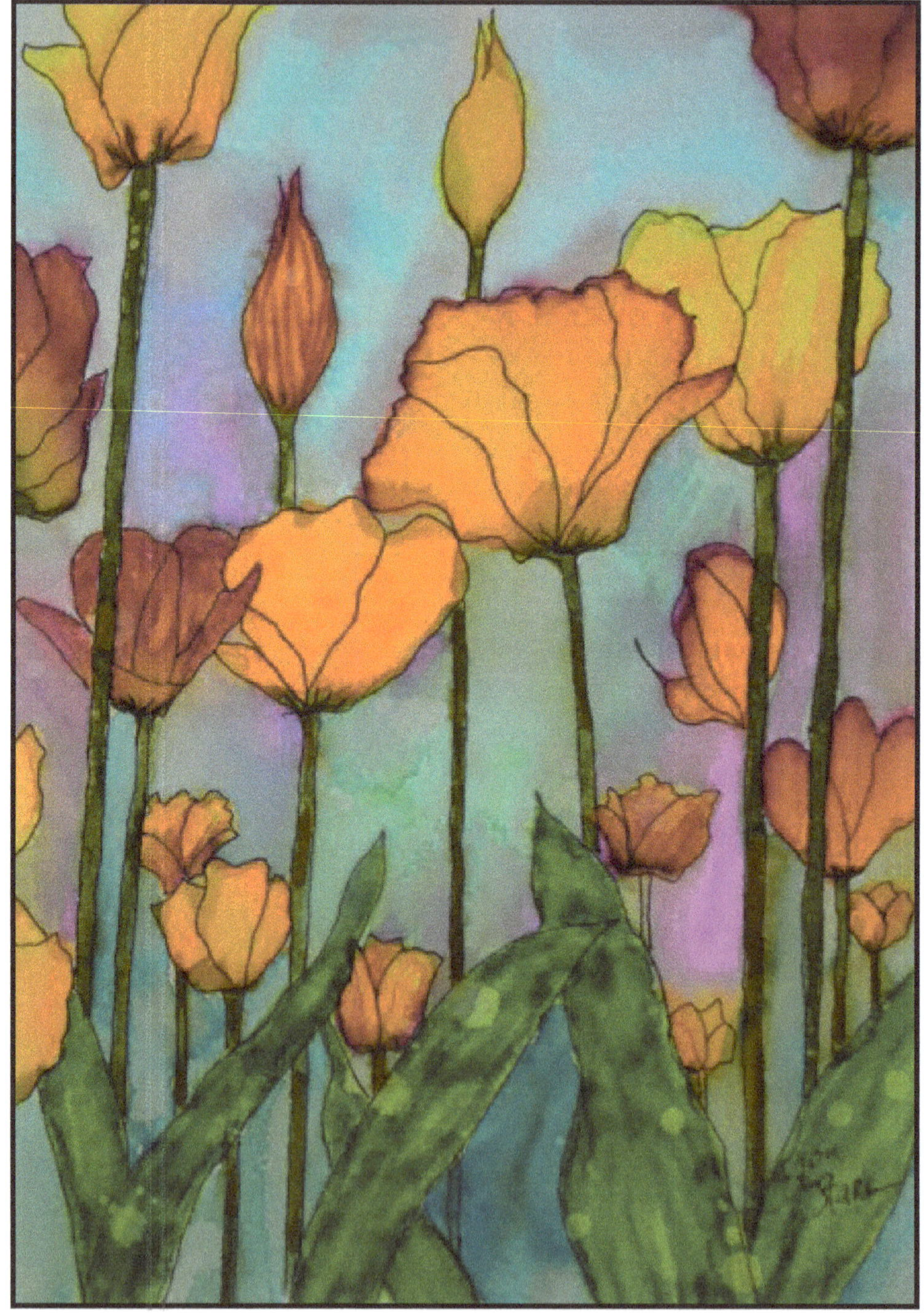

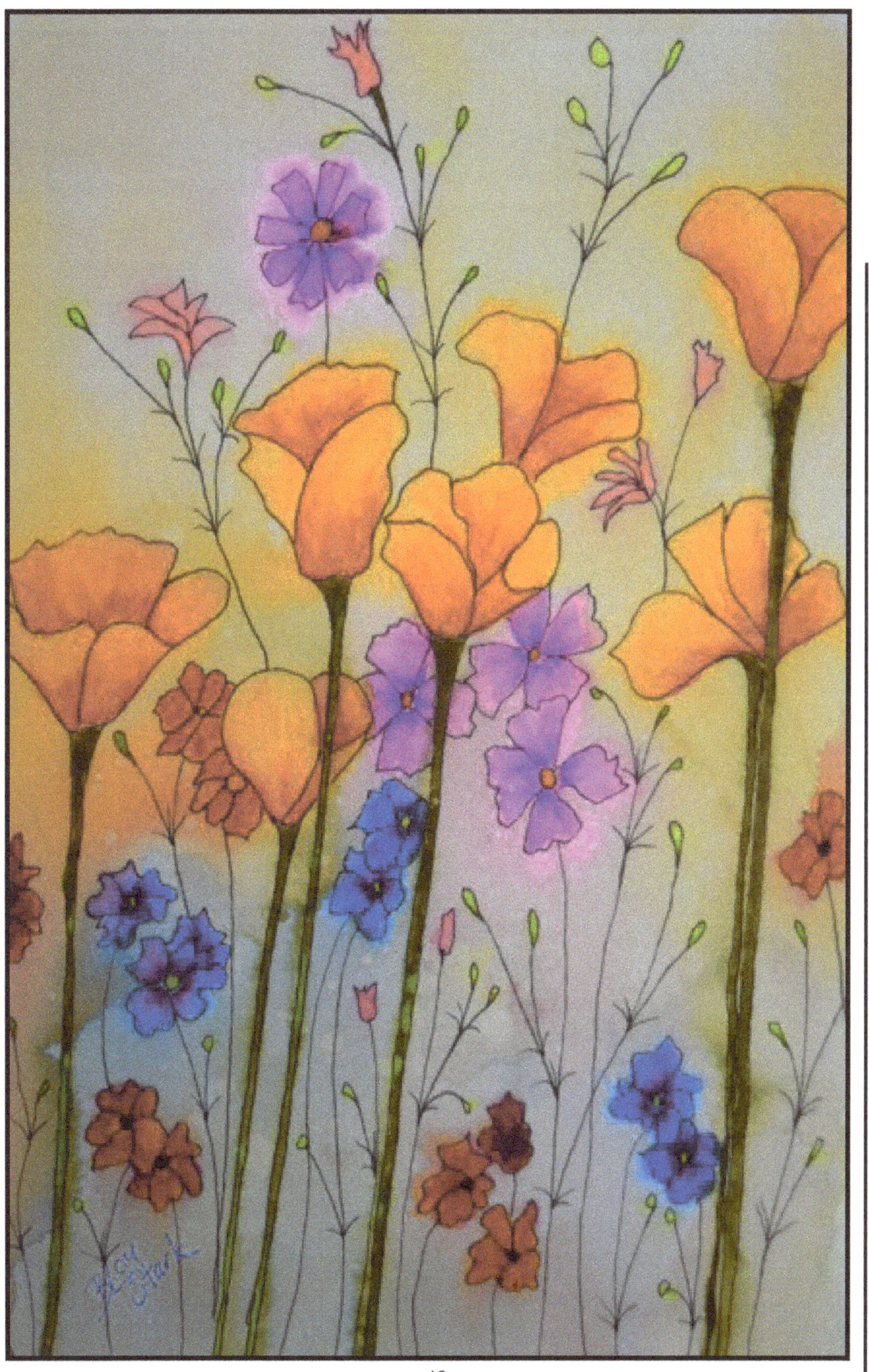

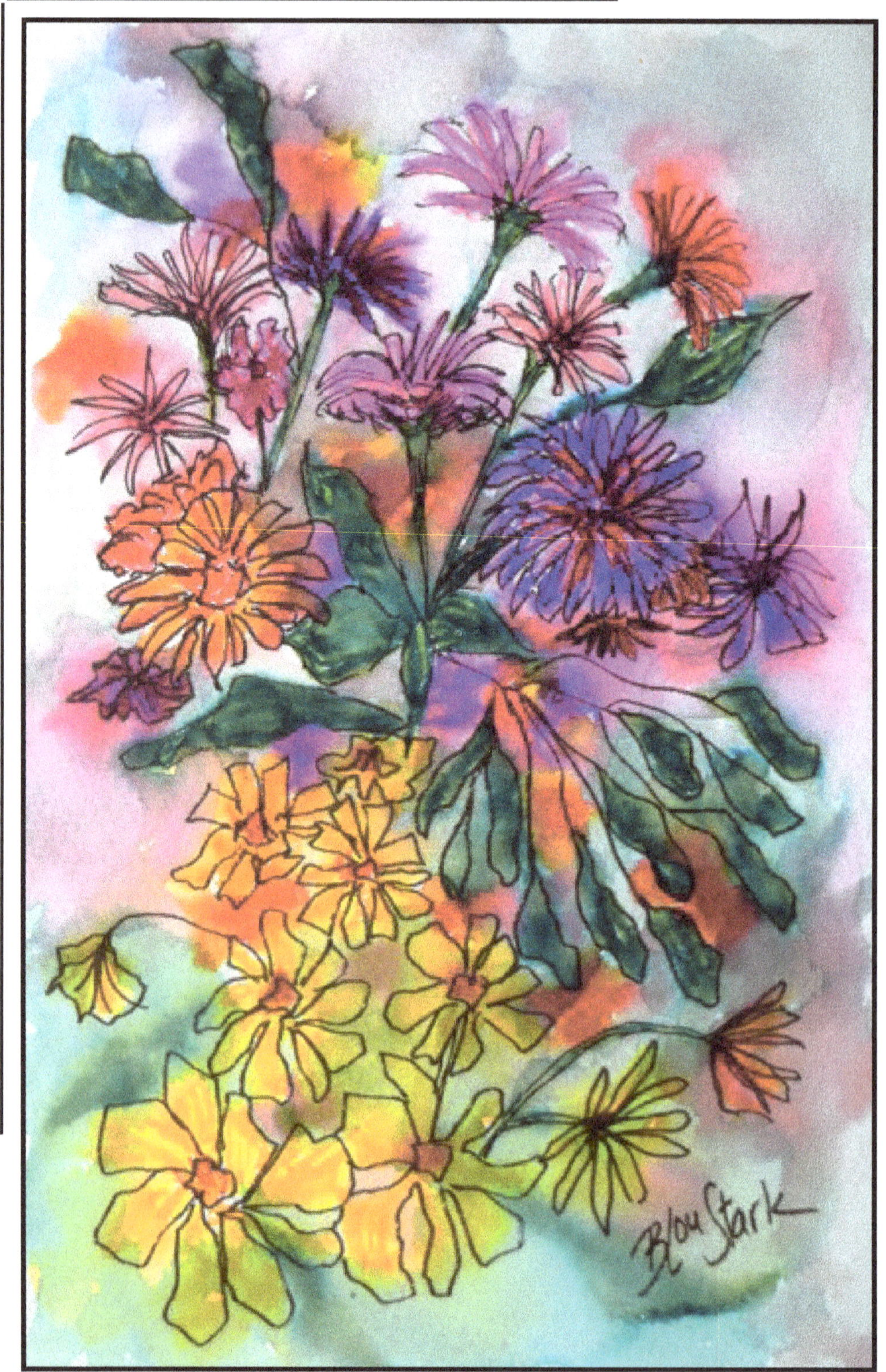
Blou Stark

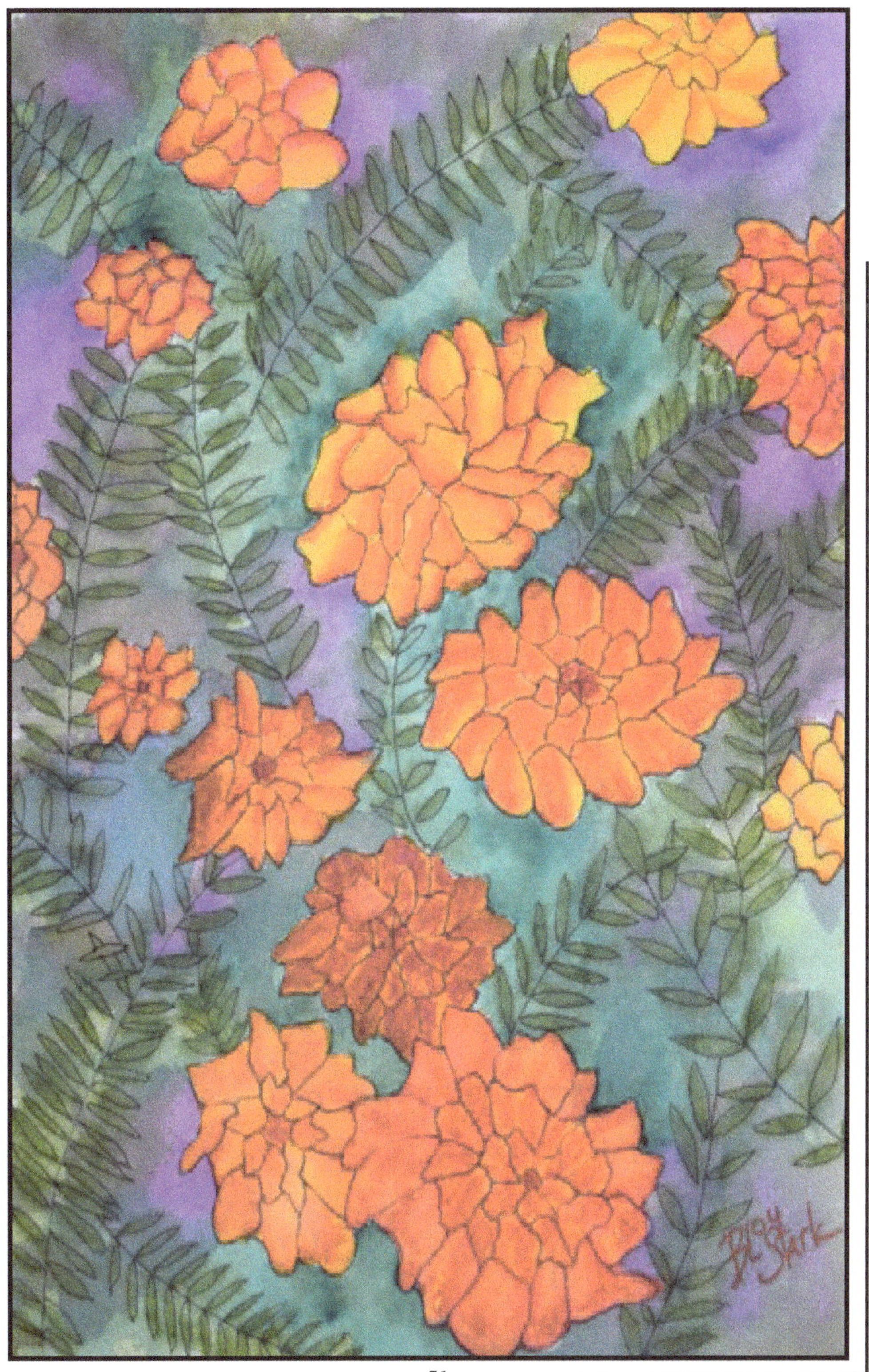

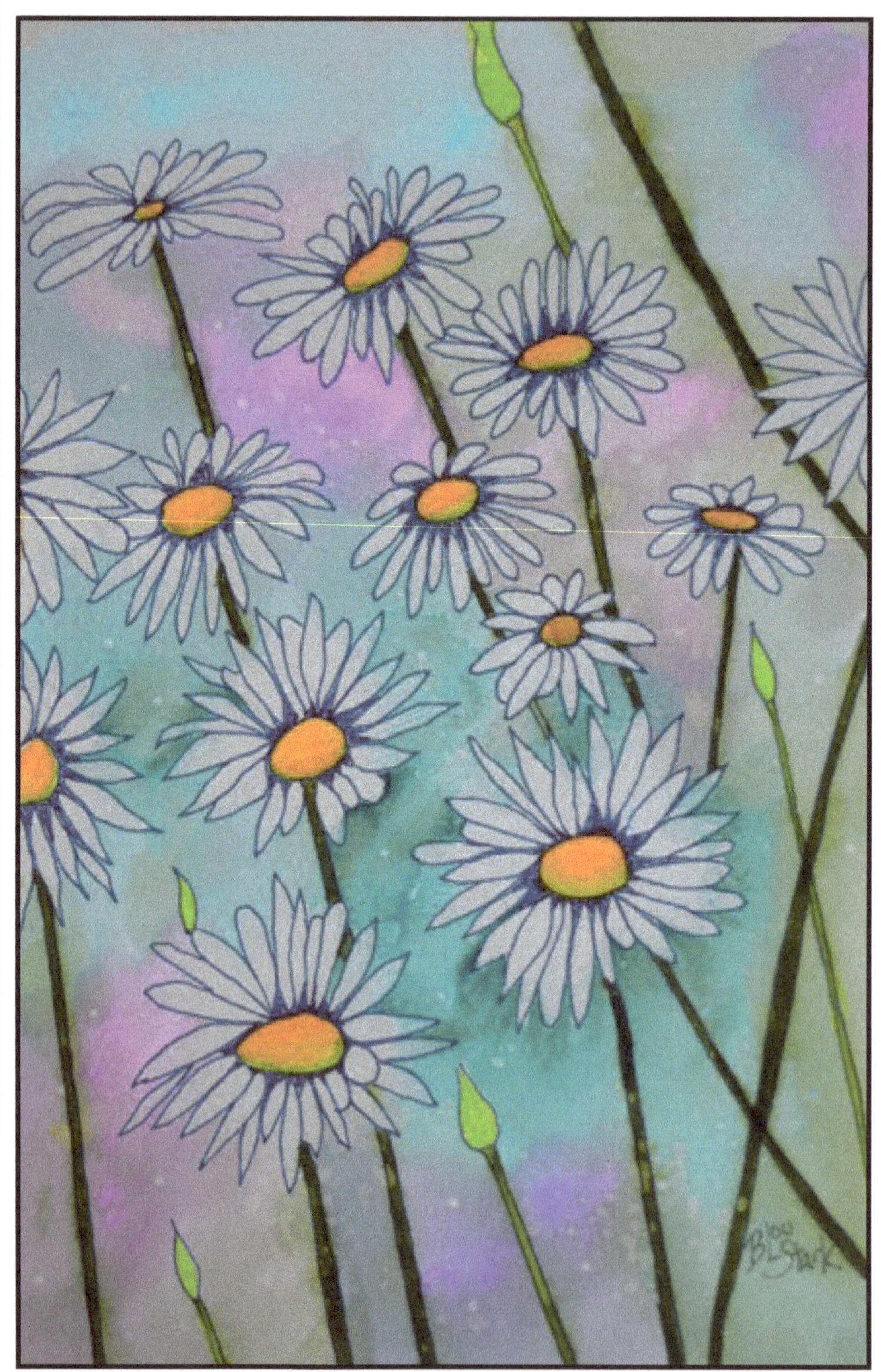

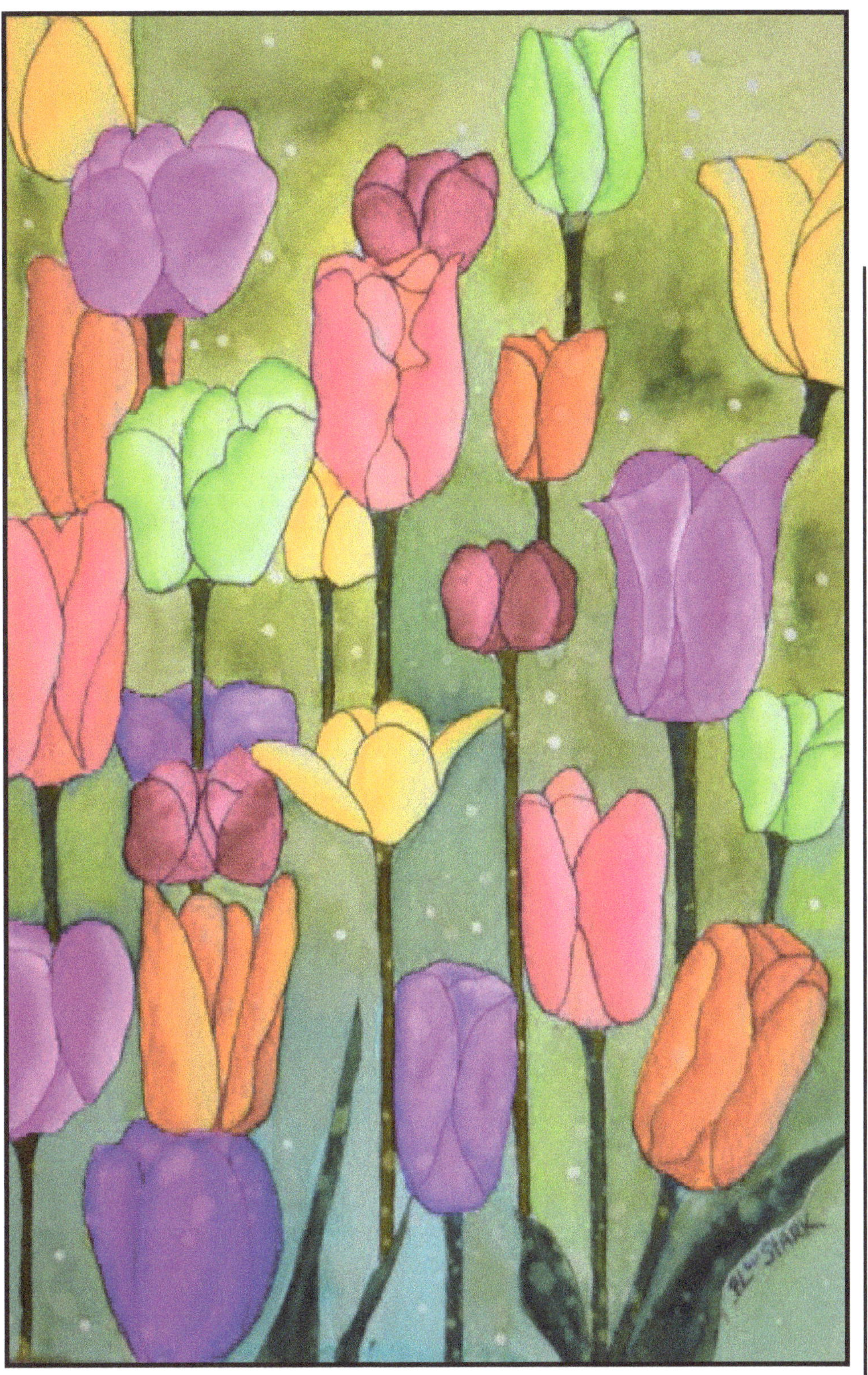

Near Light

Gina Williams

"In our leisure we reveal what kind of people we are."
--Ovid

Remember climbing trees?

Hands sticky with pitch,
ripped jeans. Spine
curved into a crook.

Ignoring hurried calls for suppertime
from below,
forgetting the grief down there.

Soothed
by the tree's embrace,
sugared sky, singing leaves.
Praying for wings.

Descent with Modification

Elena Tomorowitz

I see that
the girl with three dogs
has teeth to match, the wolf
teeth, like broken
glass, to tear
flesh-teeth it's why
they were made.

They like to share
the bowl.
Here they come.
They come for blood
or kibble – a fur monsoon,
this is what they live for.

I don't remember
a time
when all living things
were the same thing.

Everyone probably lives
like that.

Scraps of Paper

Joan Countryman

Omar was a scholar who
kept his notes on scraps
of paper when he could
or wrote with ashes on
a prison wall if that was
all he had to record
his birthplace his family
his studies in arithmetic
in philosophy, in agriculture
theology his language
his travel to foreign lands
his voyage on a great ship
across the great sea
enslaved in North America
on scraps of paper a record of
his labor in Charleston
his escape to North Carolina
his recapture in a church
in Fayetteville slips of paper
with his list of manuscripts
his notes in Arabic not
recognized by infidels
but to be found in a box
in some attic
some centuries later
People enslaved in America
learned to read and write
at their peril their teachers
considered criminals
A century later
when I read ahead in
the second-grade reader
I had to dust the closet.

Mood Cells photo project
Karyna Aslanova

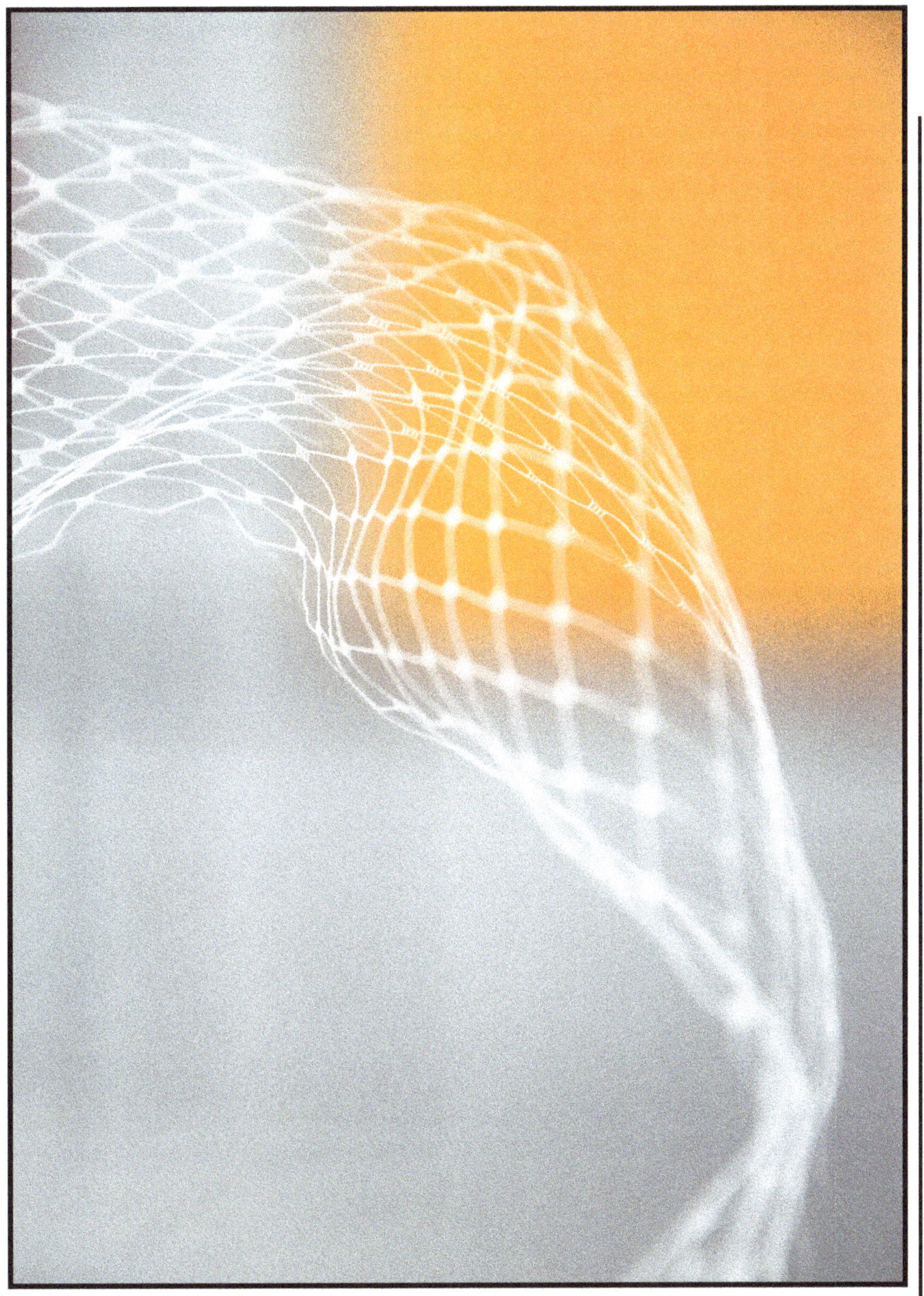

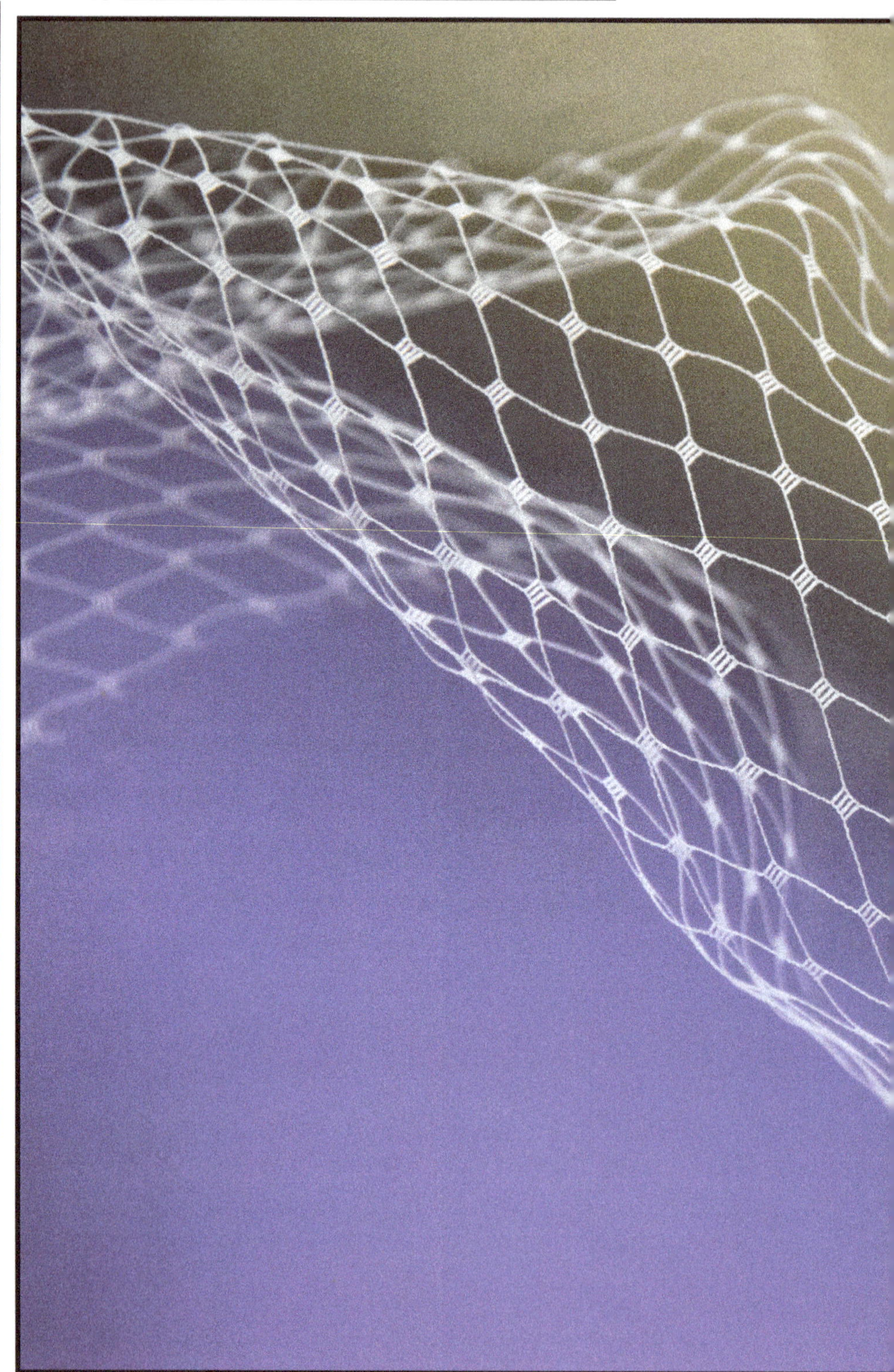

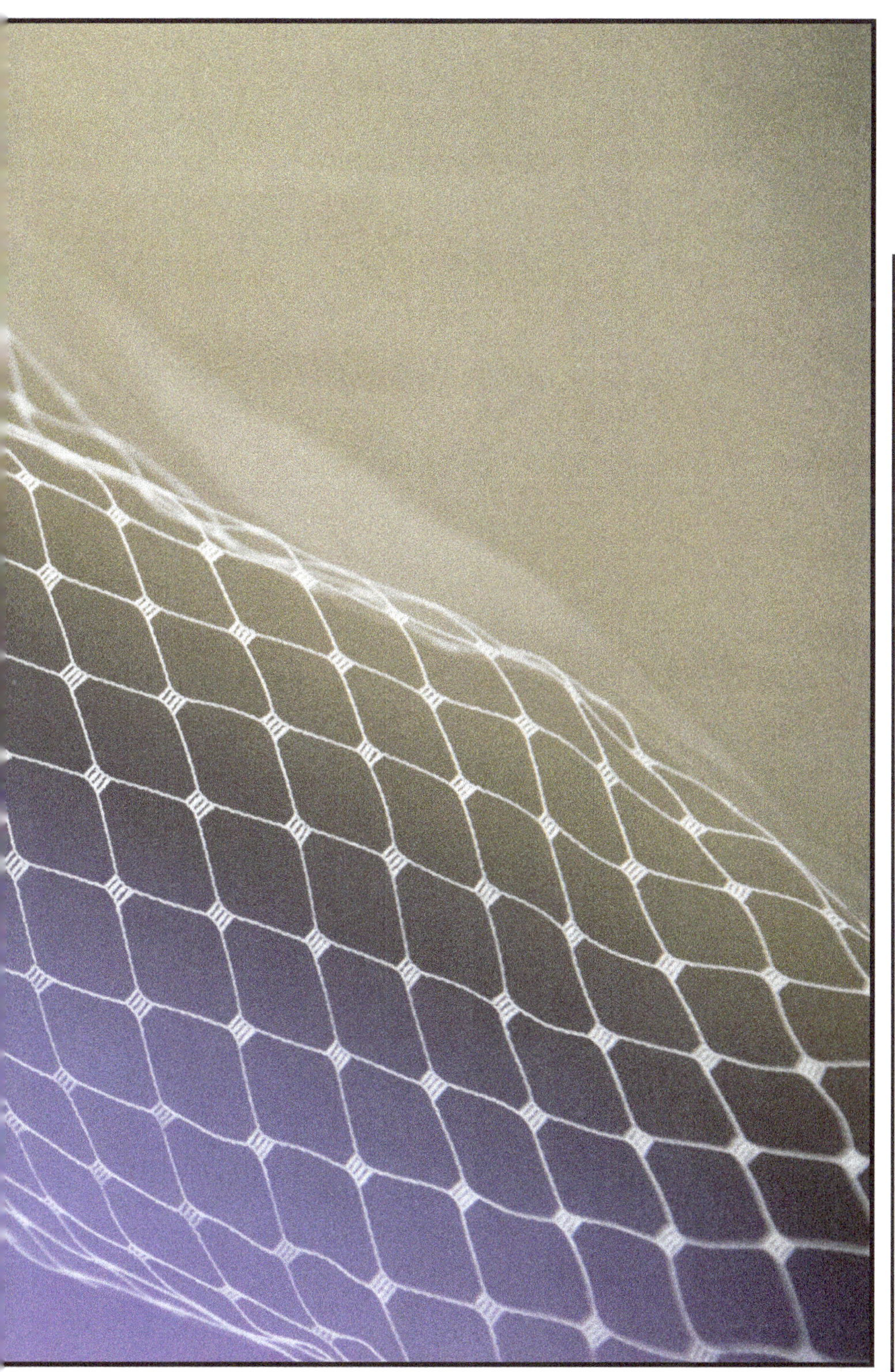

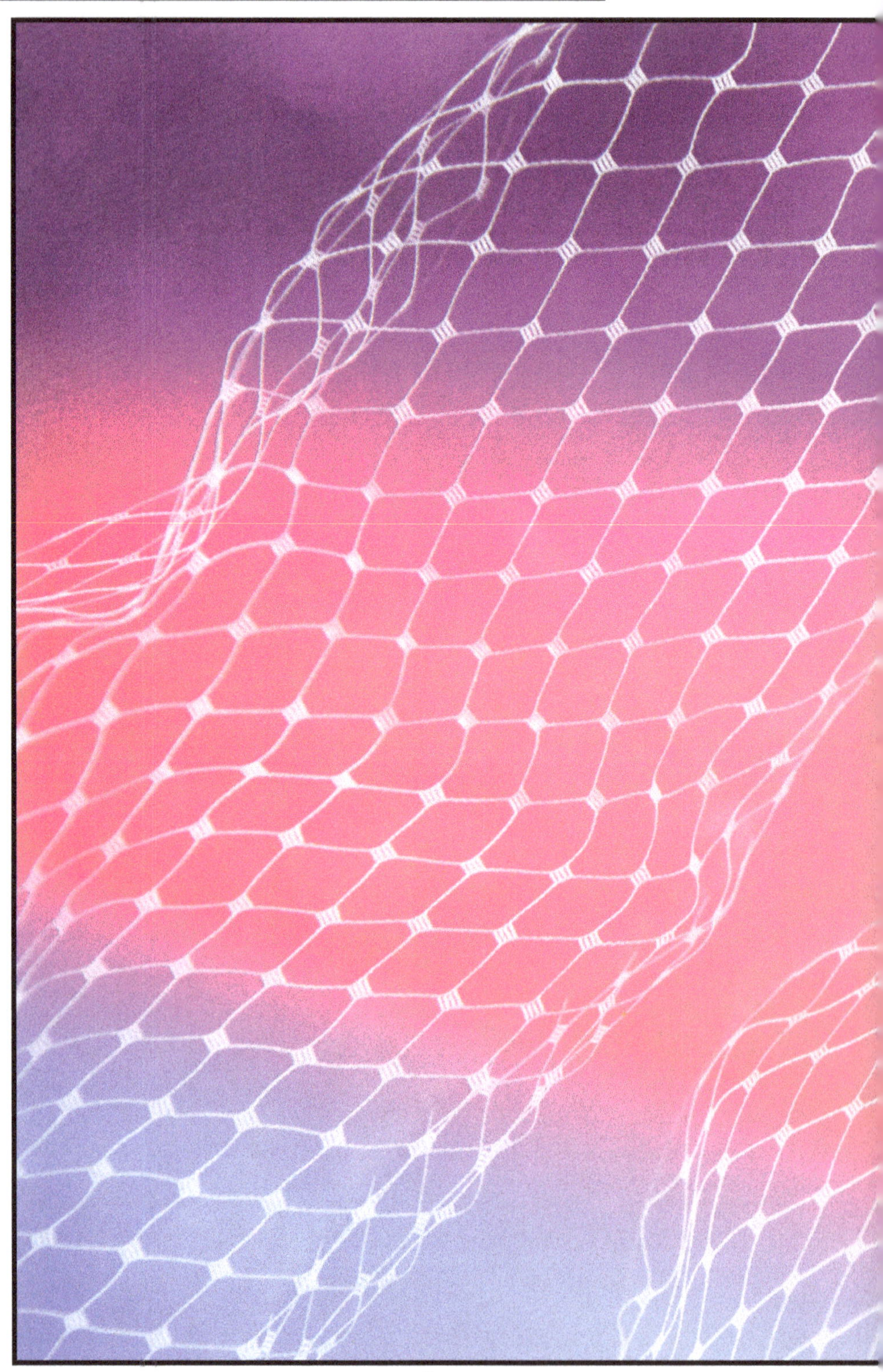

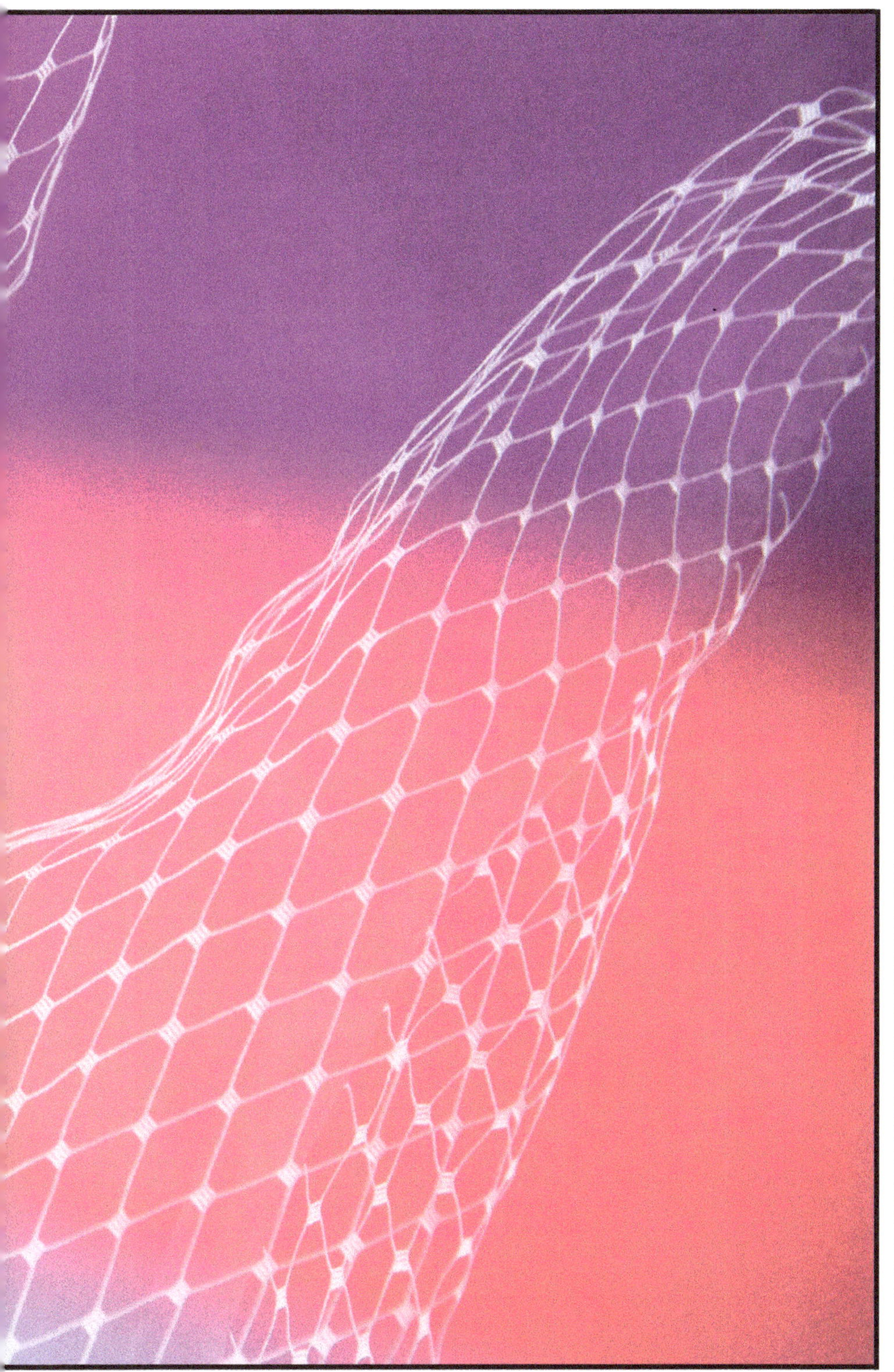

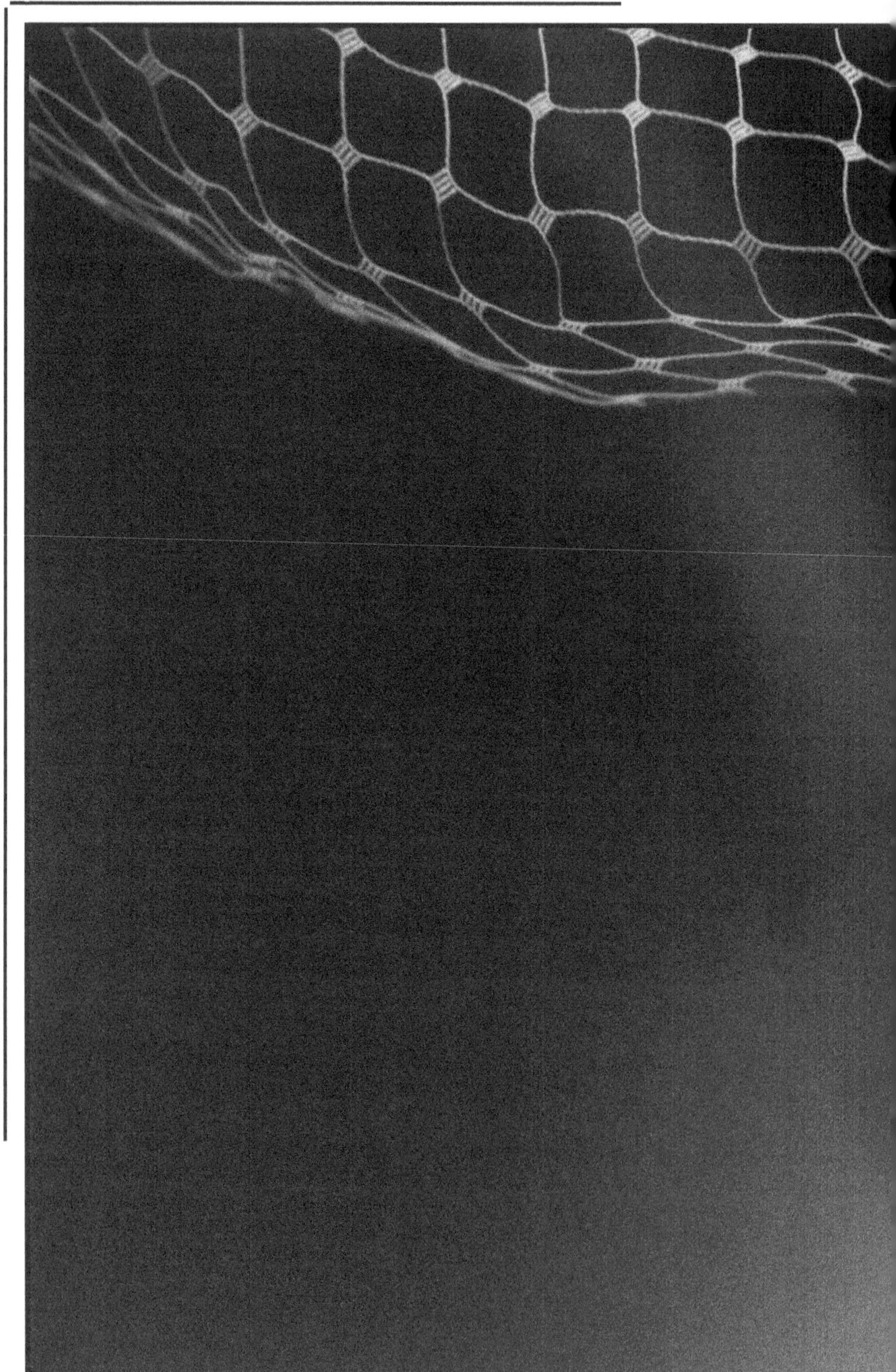

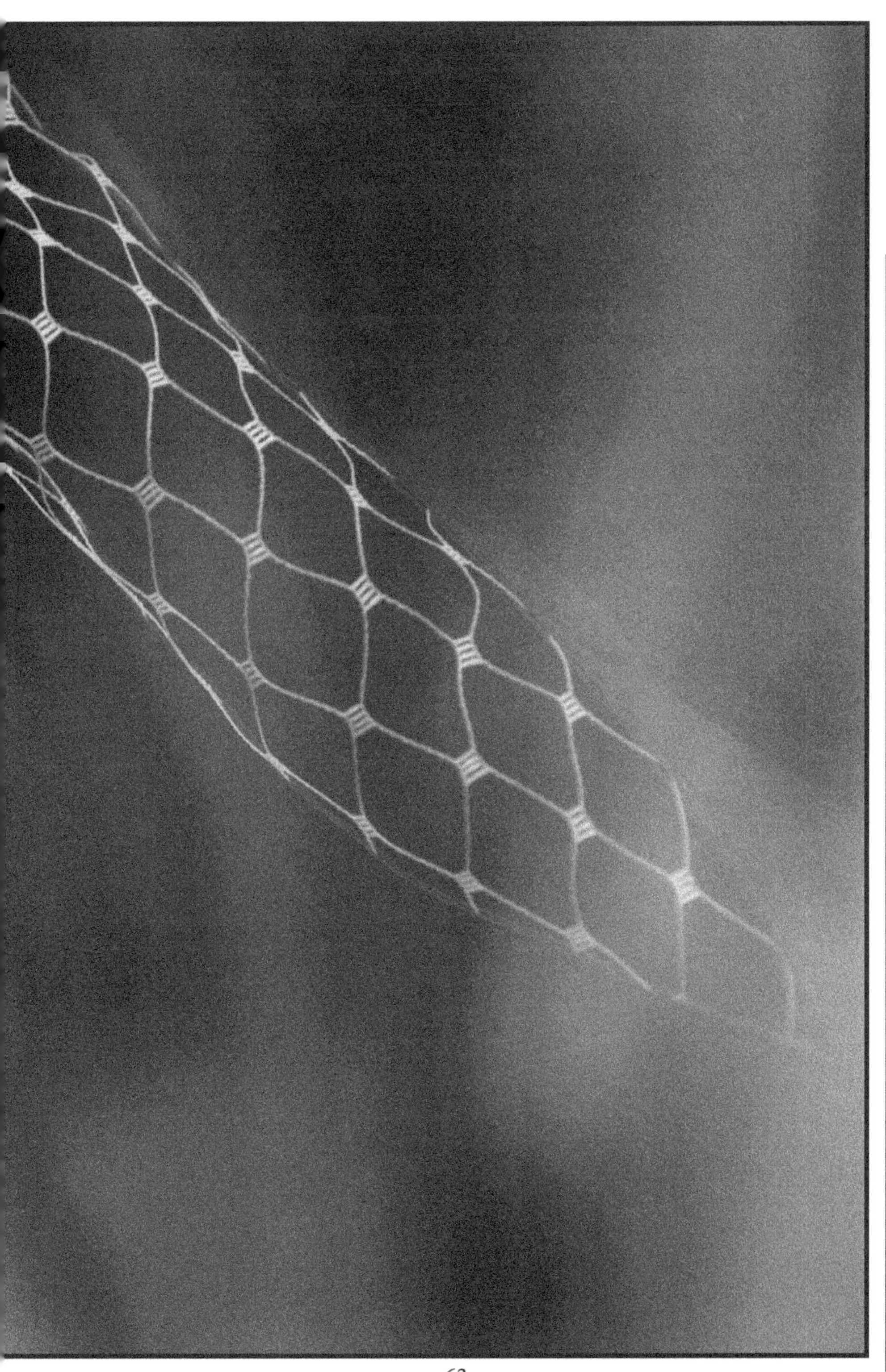

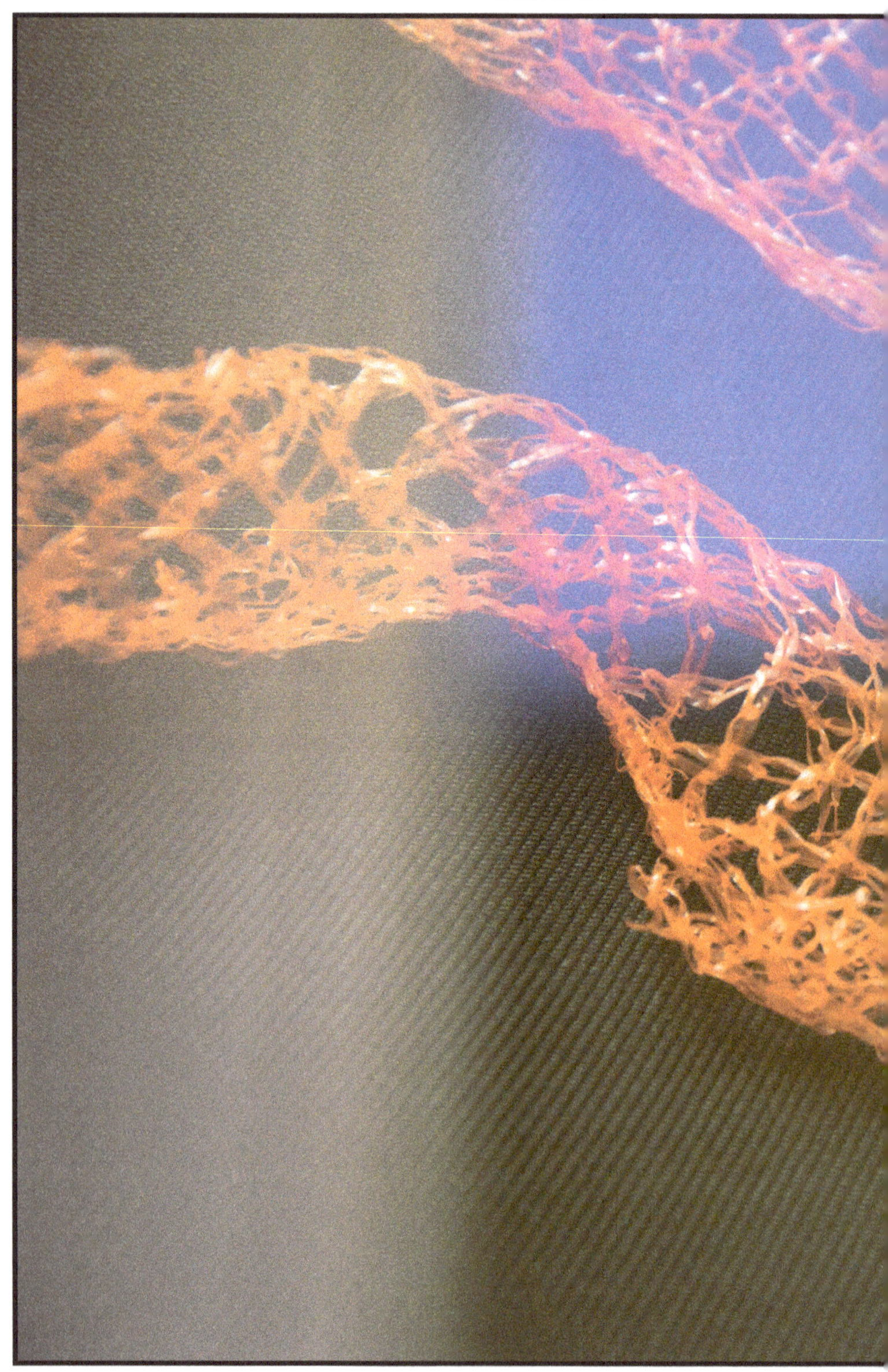

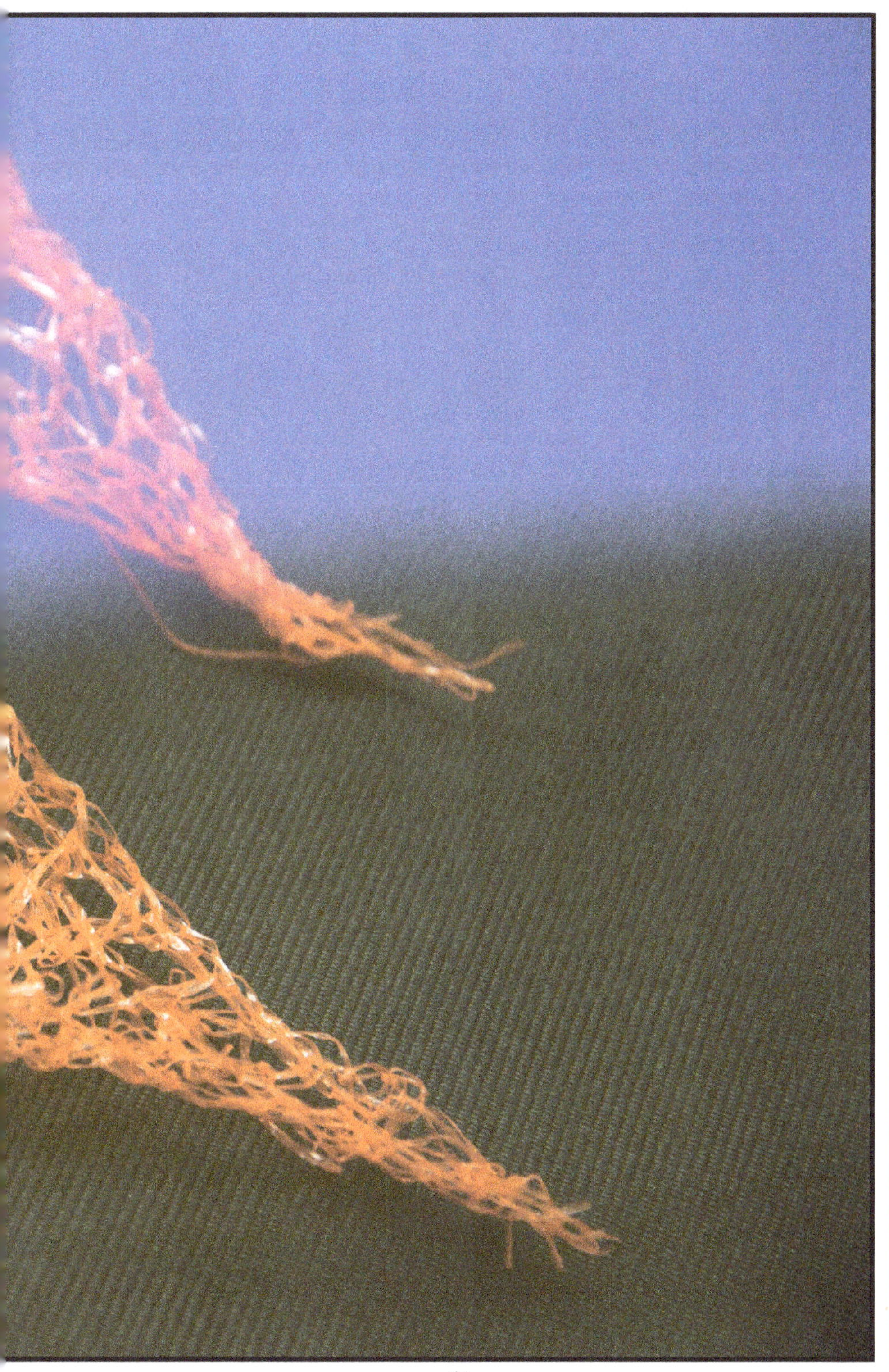

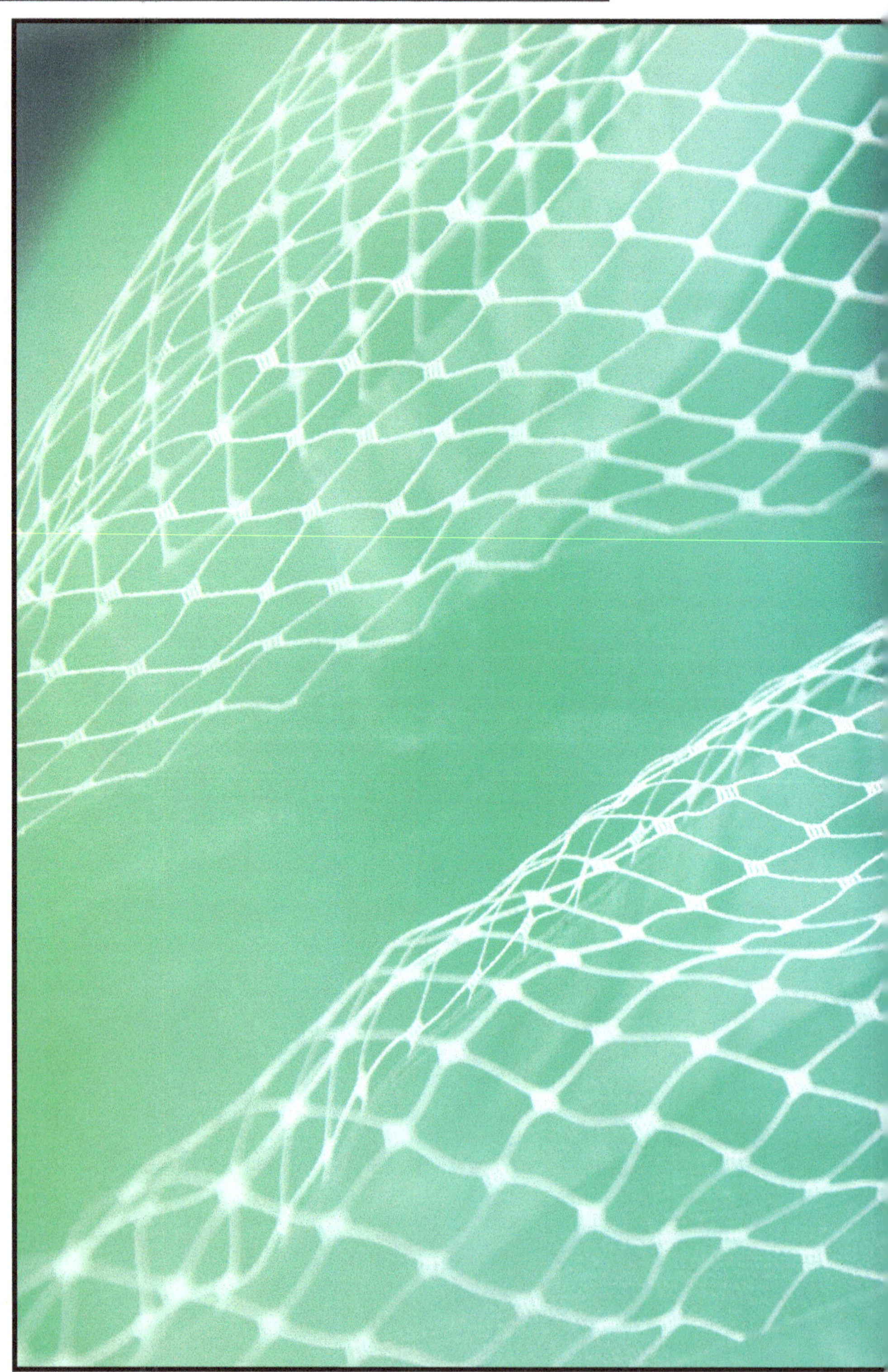

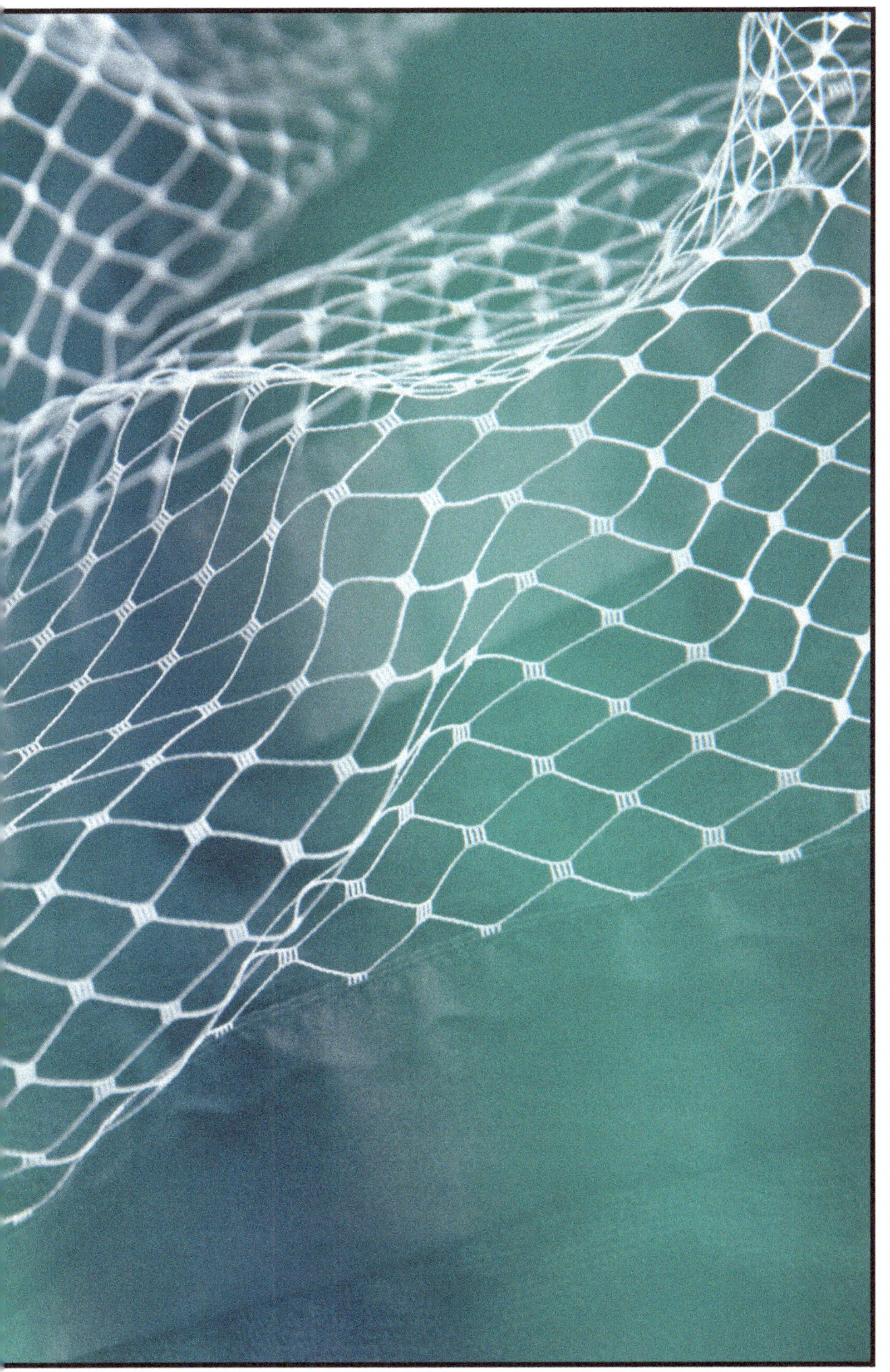

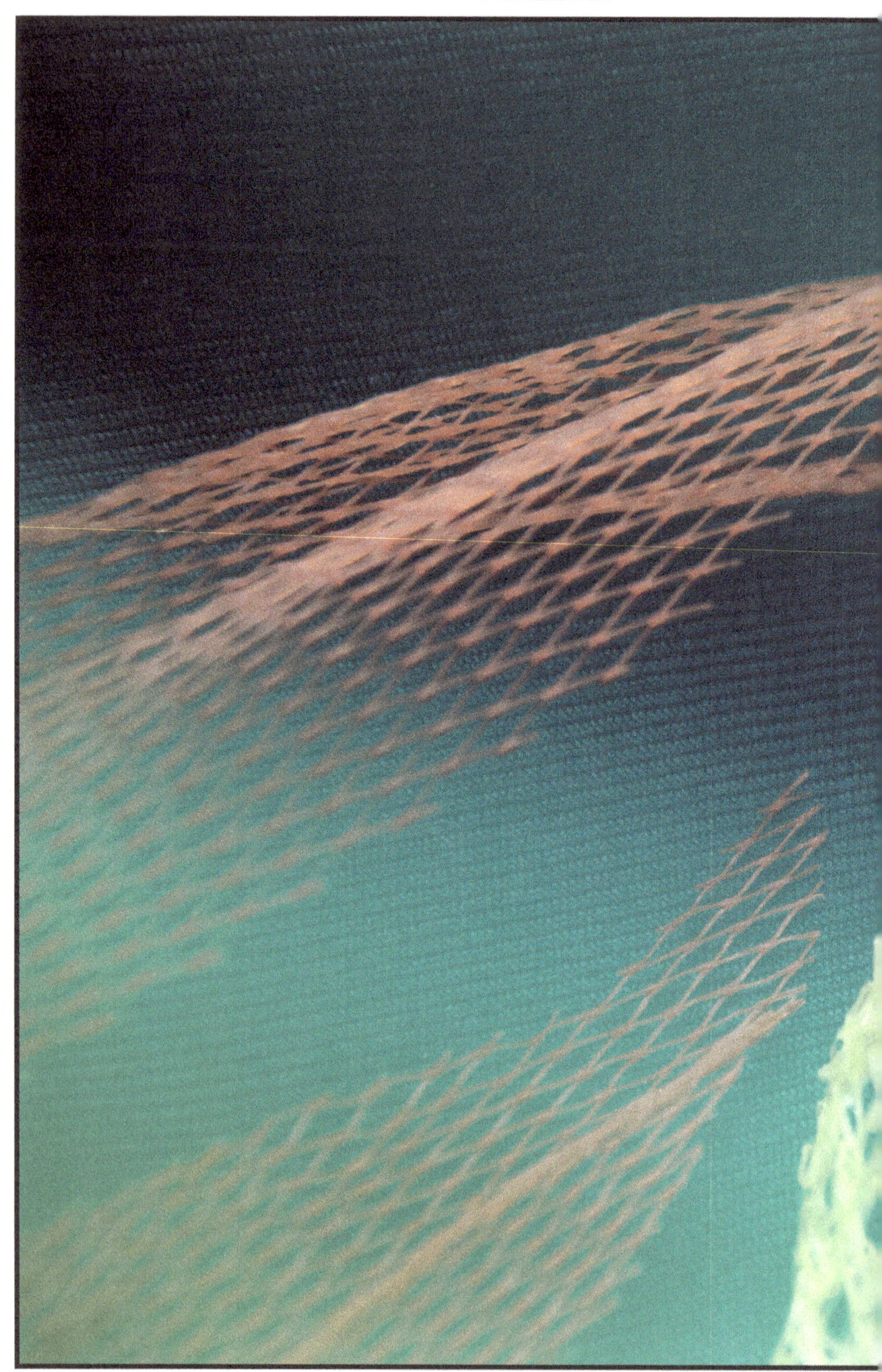

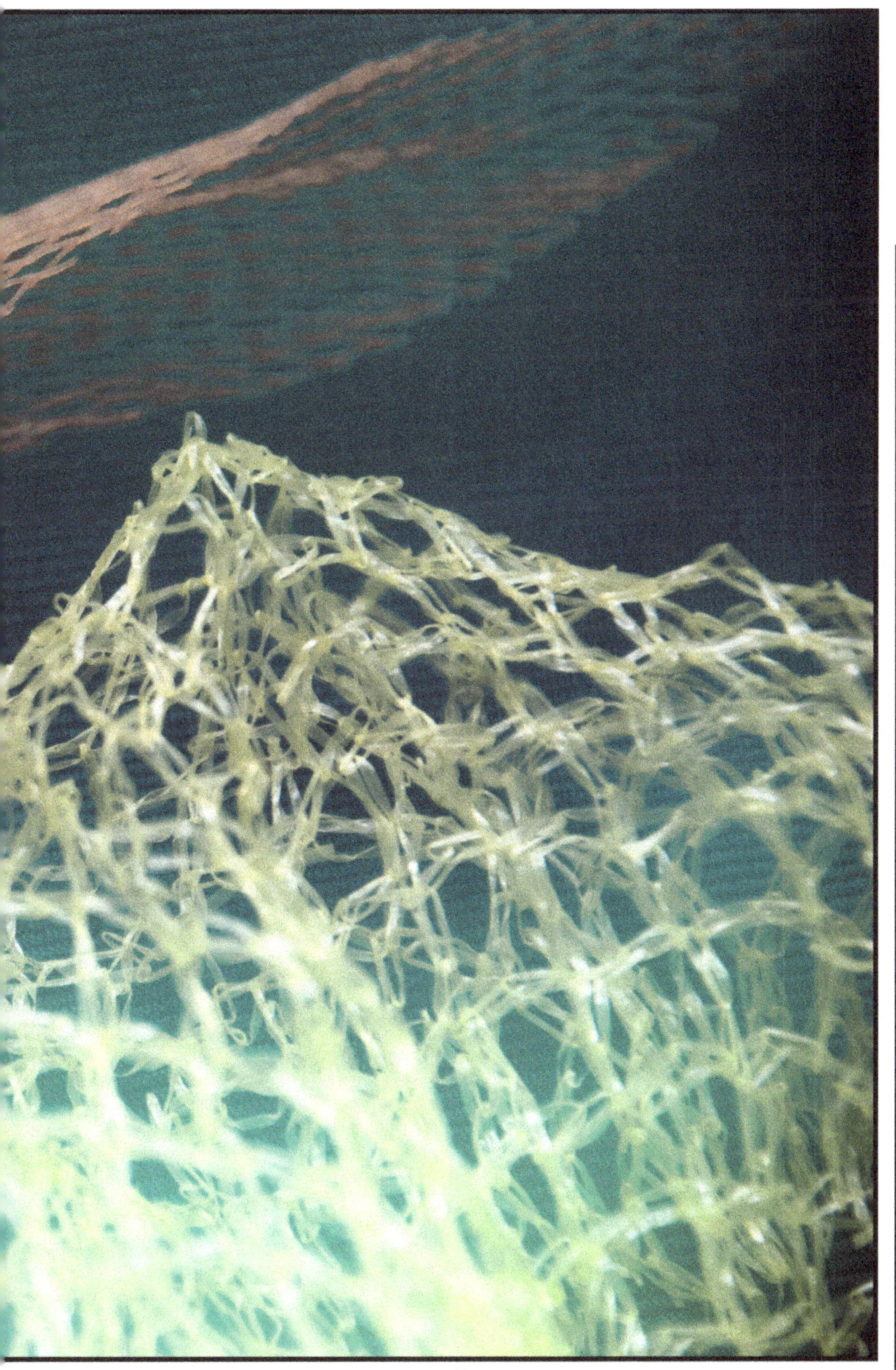

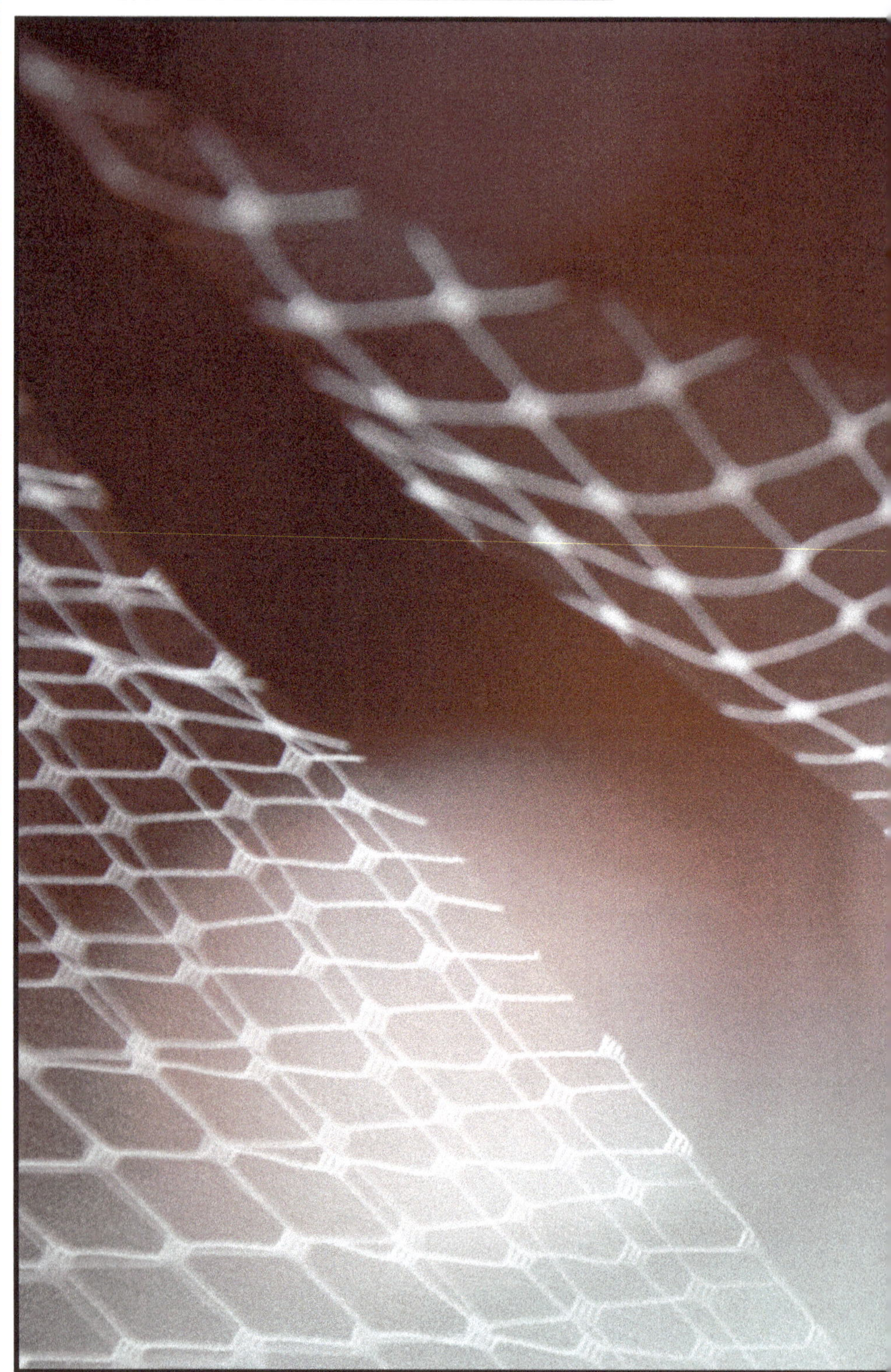

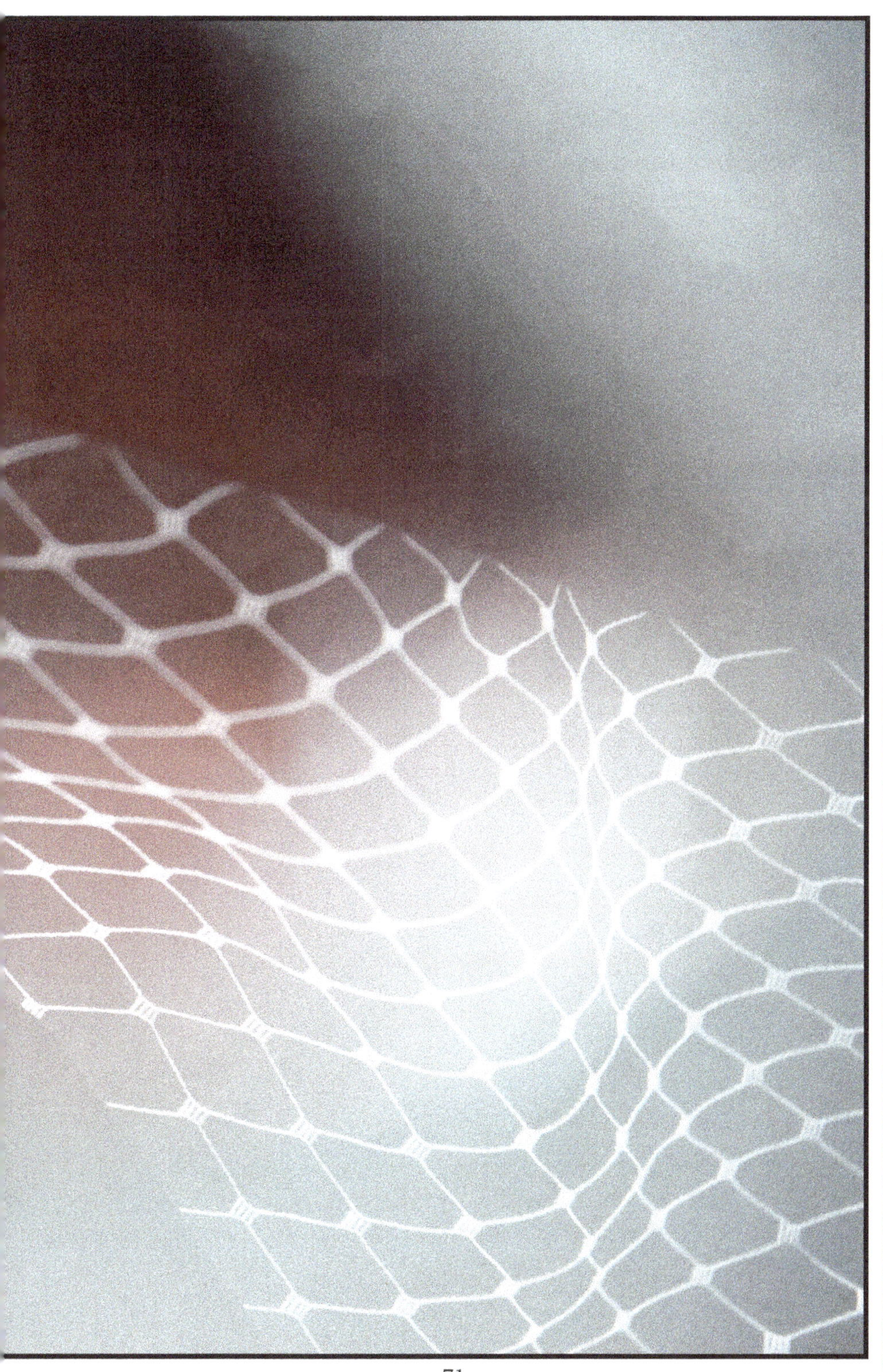

Dalida

Peggy Hammond

In Paris, a bust of Dalida
Punctuates the singer's neighborhood,
Marks a large love.

The bronze likeness, silent watcher,
Wears well its darkness,
Except the rounded breasts

Which gleam golden on
Cloud-cloaked afternoon.
Passersby, looking for luck,

Or boys wanting practice,
Have rubbed and robbed them
Of their nut-brown hue.

Dalida, with half-lidded eyes fixed
On space that rests above mortal plane,
Forgives this familiarity.

Her house reveals this moment's tenant
With one open window, the curtain undulating,
A sheer belly dancer, on December drafts.

But in the past, this tower home watched
Love's crests and falls,
Watched glittering awards and fame

Fail to delight the soul it tried to sustain,
Watched Dalida write words to break
The world's faithful heart.

No longer could she resist shadows
And mists that rise on further shore.
No longer could she move as goddess

On paths of this world. In May's soft glow
When all others woke to life fresh and bright,
She set her course Sunward.

Leaving Earthbound humans unable to follow,
Mourning after her like Zeus
After Io.

INSECTALIA

Julia Muench

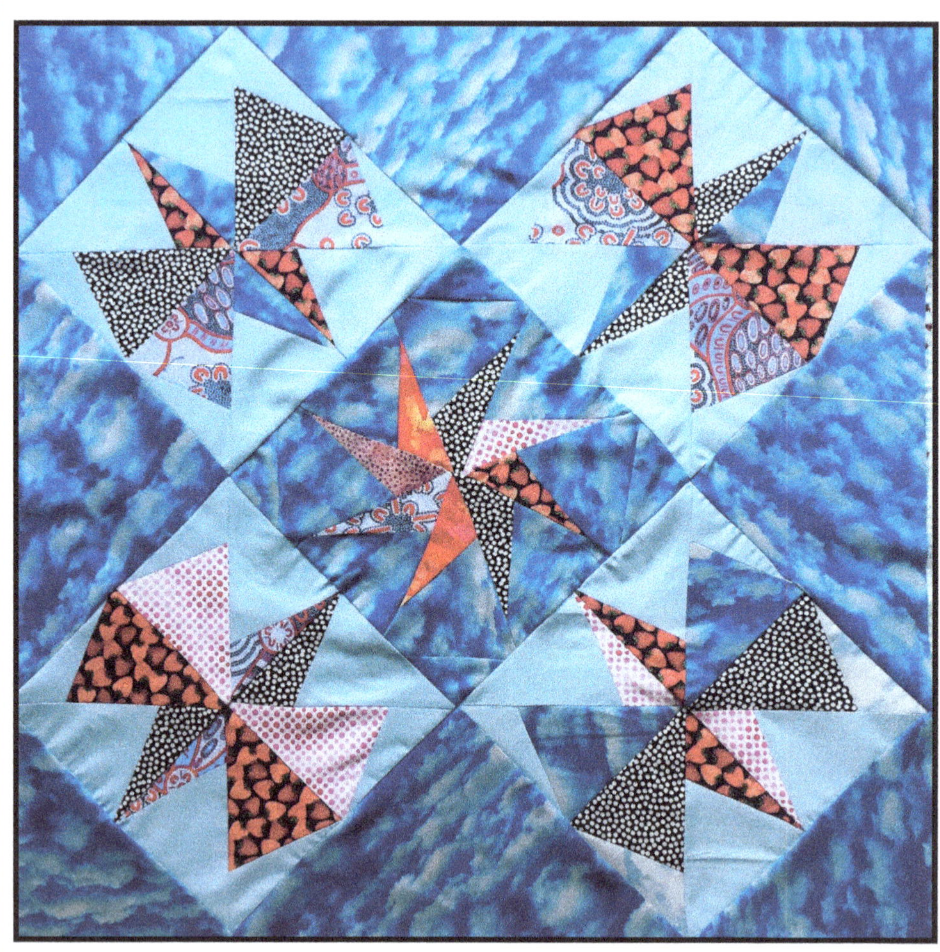

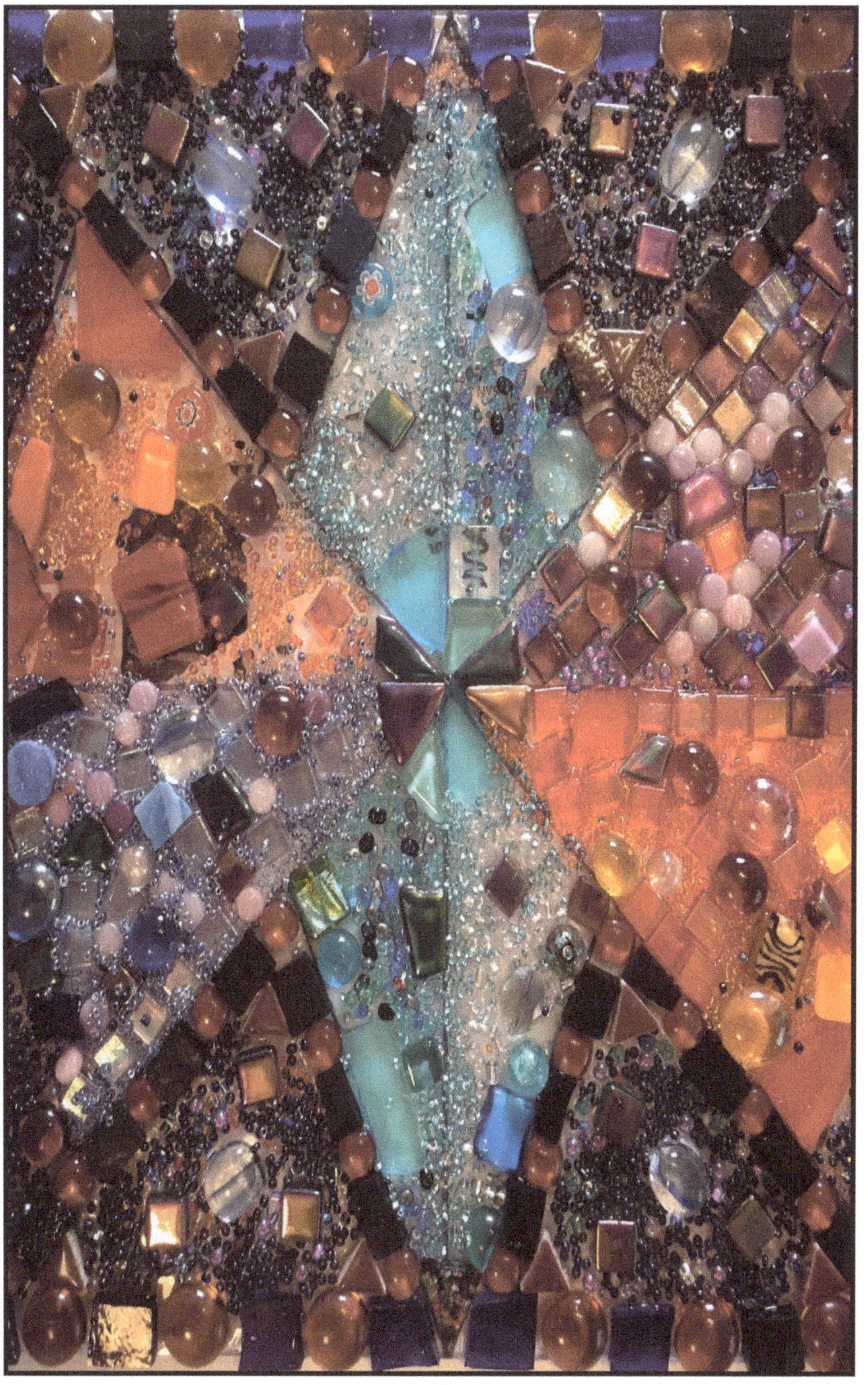

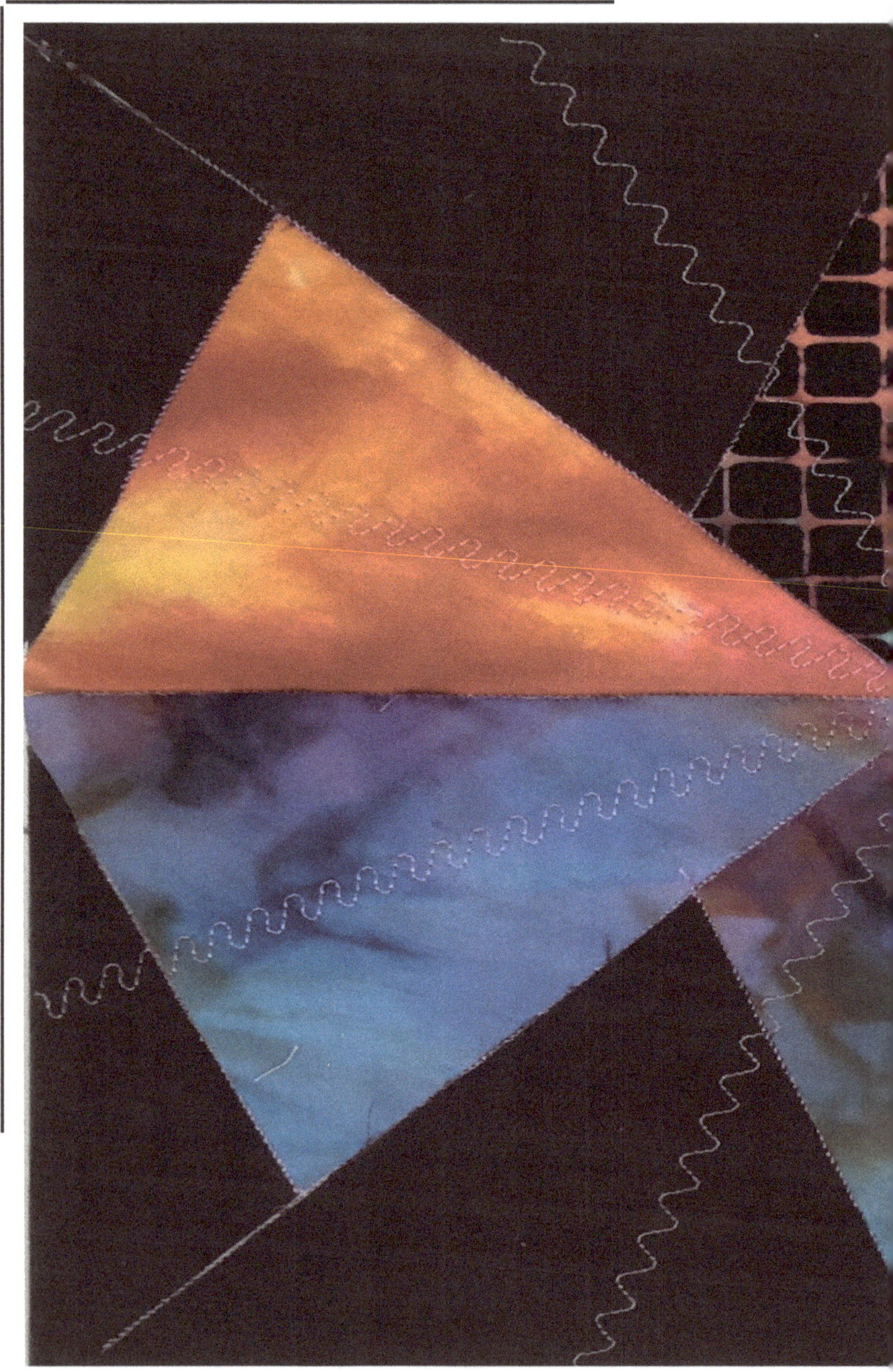

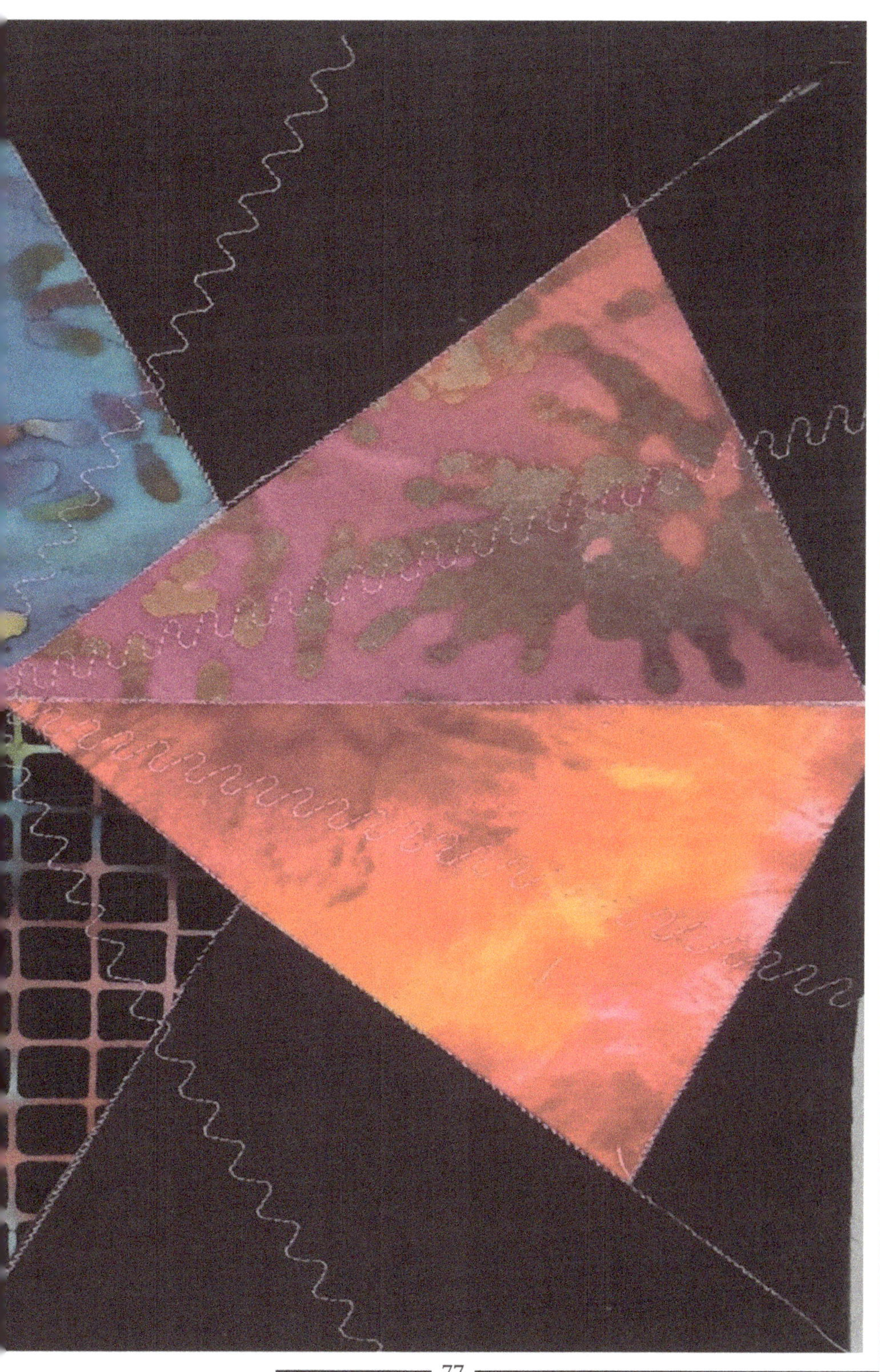

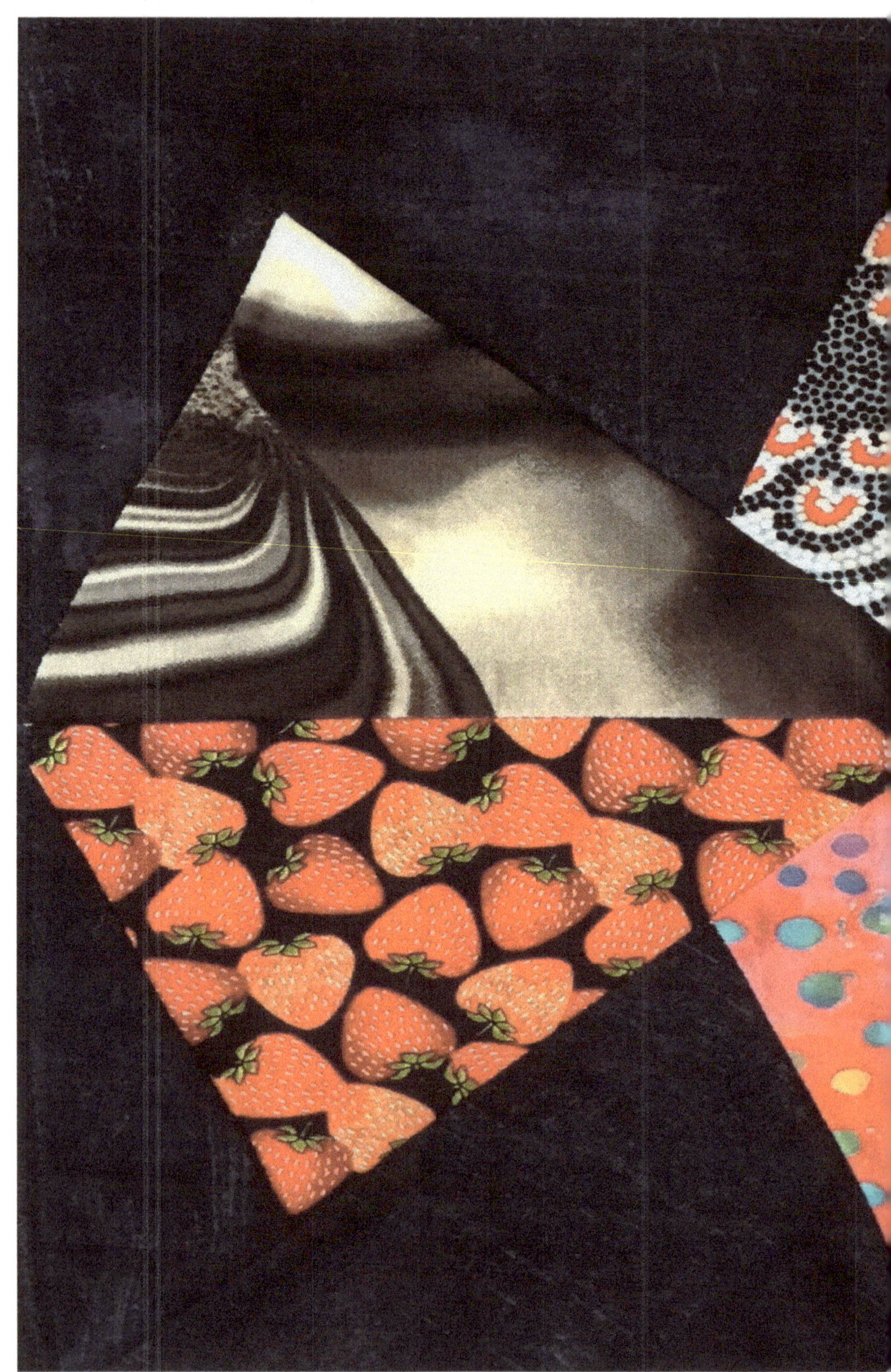

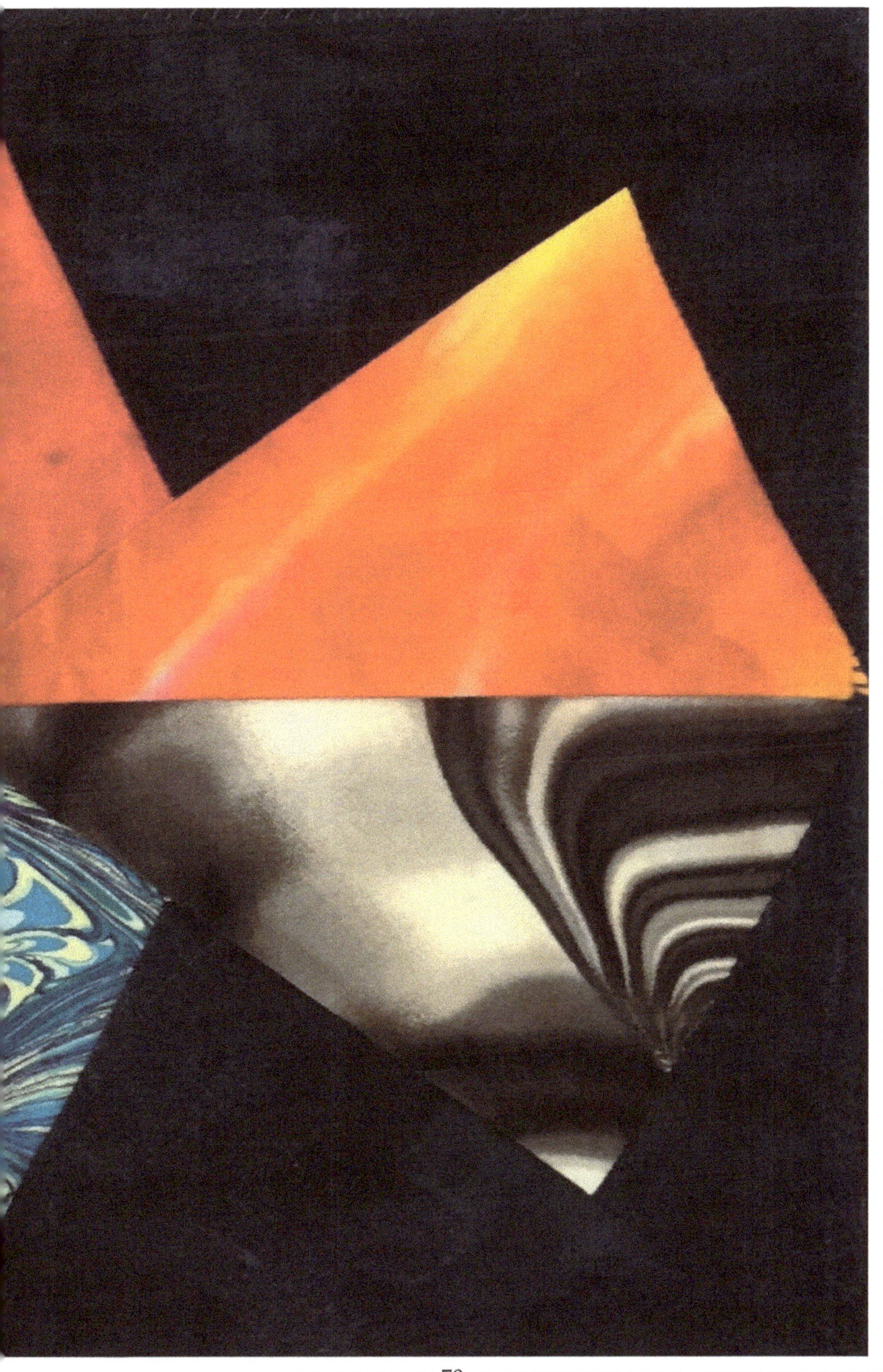

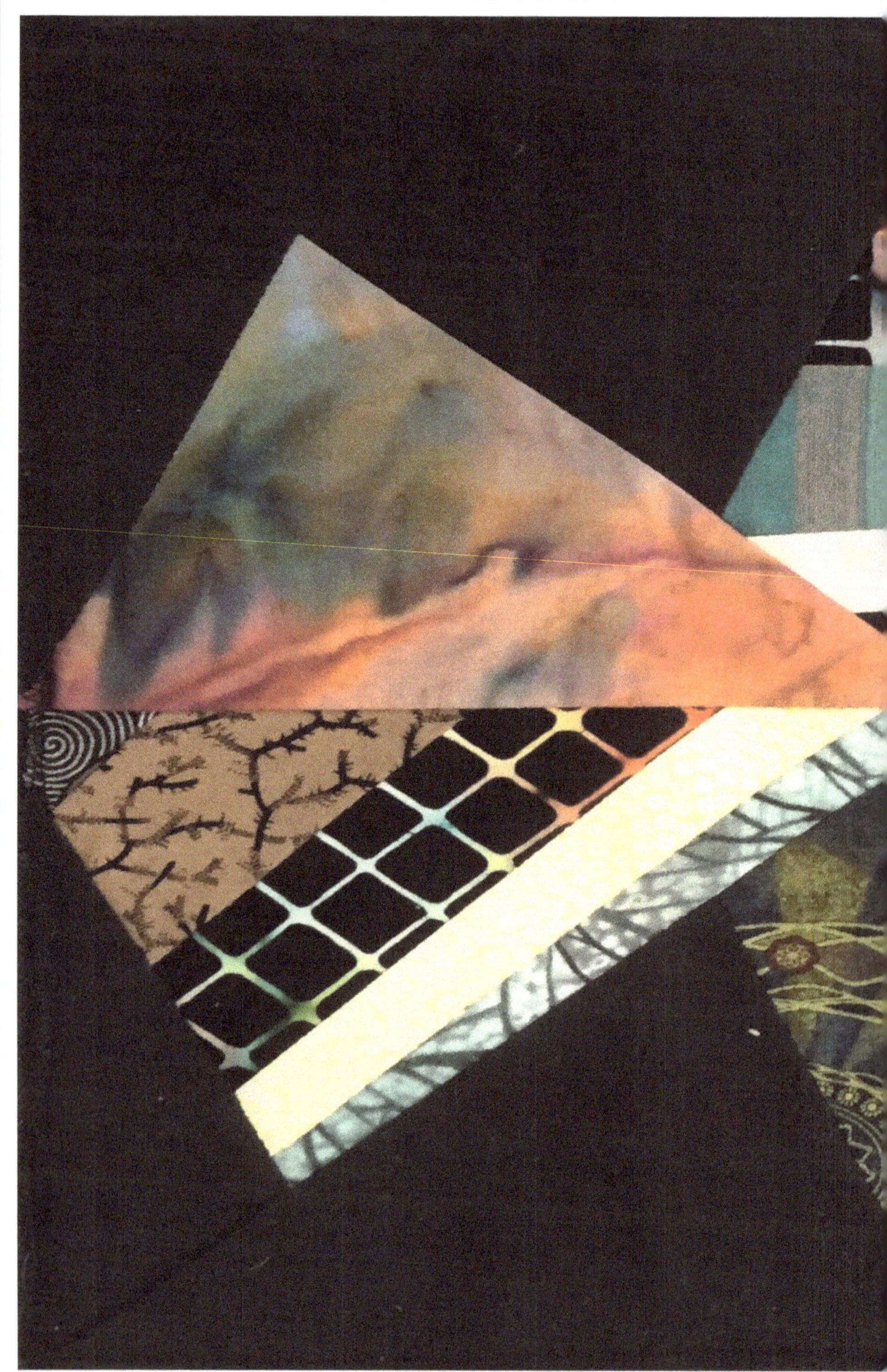

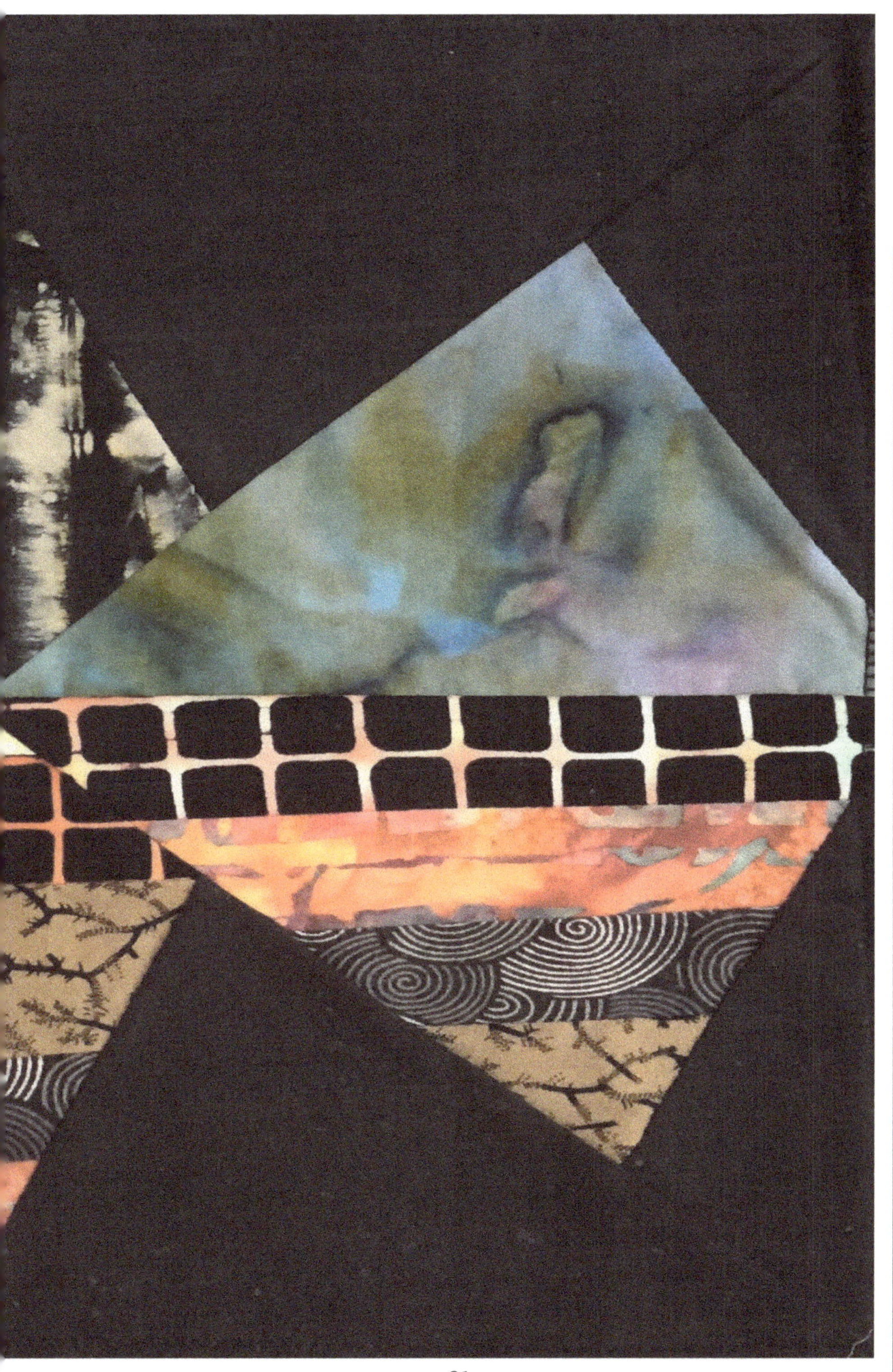

Another Duel

rlongfield

With Apologies to Eugene Field

The shamrock-print dog, and the kelly-co cat,
On opposite ends of the pressroom sat,
With the dog at the lectern, and the cat in the back,
Each on their haunches, prepared for attack.
It was nearly nine, (or so I heard)
And neither one had uttered a word—
The ghosts of James Brady, and ole Jody Powell,
Concurred in opinion, with mutual scowl,
That the morning's event would never end well,
With the dog and cat aiming, the best story to tell,
To finally determine, for once and for all,
Whose public pronouncements, gave greater appall.
(Forgive me if I sound too bitter, I am merely repeating
What I read on Twitter!)

The shamrock-print dog began to howl,
The kelly-co cat cried —foul!—foul!—foul!
And in one leap, was on the stage—
The shamrock- print dog, consumed with rage,
Chased the kelly-co cat around the room,
While all the while, their words of doom,
Their alternative facts, and fake news spewed,
With odor, like poisonous coffee brewed,
Its acrid scent, wafted throughout the air,
And left all reporters, slumped in their chairs.
(Excuse me if I sound deranged, even Jody's hair
was rearranged!)

Mr. Brady was beside himself—
"Why was there no taser, why was there no shelf
To surreptitiously remove from a wall,
To end this great misery, for once and for all?"
But the shamrock-print dog, and the kelly-co cat,

Intent on more havoc, went this way and that—
Strands of bleached blonde ano-hair,
Were mixed with the fur of a soviet bear—
An amulet worn by the shamrock-print dog,
Given in secret, under cover of fog,
(Don't quote me on this, I only repeat
What was told to me by anonymous Tweet!)

By the end of an hour, the room was in tatters,
The lecturn upended, and glass goblets shattered;
The White House picture was on the floor,
The flag barely standing, nothing left of the door,
The room almost empty, the reporters long gone,
Except for one pro, whose work was not done—
It was Mara Liaison, from NPR,
Who gathered the remnants, from near and from far,
Of the dog and the cat, who could not agree,
On who was the best maker of fake history.
"We all tried to warn you..." our dear Mara said,
As she swept them up, from toe to head.
(Pease don't fancy, that I am waxing shady,
I heard that part from Powell and Brady!)

"Even artificial intelligence robots face stereotypical sexism in the workplace"

Kelly O'Rourke

As the New York Times pointed out
last year, various email inbox assistants are called
Clara, Amy, Julie, Crystal, Jeannie, Cloe, Dawn, and Donna.

Siri, Alexa, help desk robo-voices and our GPS navigation
systems all perform what are essentially service tasks,
administrative roles typically associated with women.

People prefer to hear a masculine-sounding voice
from a leader, according to research —
so Watson got a male voice.

The Spot also includes Amazon's ESP feature,
so that only the Echo device closest to you
will respond to your command

(key if you're living
with multiple Alexa
devices under one roof).

(Little) Henry also said the cool thing about Alexa
is that "she is one of those kind of electronics
that gets smarter and smarter the more you use her."

"Even artificial intelligence robots face stereotypical sexism in the workplace" borrows its title from a news article of the same name by Olivia Goldhill published on May 15, 2016 on www.qz.com. Lines from several other pieces by Ry Crist, Kurt Schlosser, Chandra Steele and Marie Glenn are borrowed for this poem.

Sources Directly Cited

Even artificial intelligence robots face stereotypical sexism in the workplace. By Olivia Goldhill, May 15, 2016. https://qz.com/684879/even-artificial-intelligence-robots-face-stereotypical-sexism-in-the-workplace/

Amazon Echo Spot review: Alexa's touchscreen misses the sweet spot. By Ry Crist, January 16, 2018. https://www.cnet.com/reviews/amazon-echo-spot-review/

Boy meets artificial girl: My son got an Echo Dot, and here's what he's saying to Amazon's Alexa. By Kurt Schlosser, March 20, 2017.
https://www.geekwire.com/2017/boy-meets-artificial-girl-son-got-echo-dot-heres-hes-saying-amazons-alexa/

The Real Reason Voice Assistants Are Female (and Why it Matters). By Chandra Steele, January 29, 2018. https://medium.com/pcmag-access/the-real-reason-voice-assistants-are-female-and-why-it-matters-e99c67b93bde

Few good men: Why is the growing population of AI voices predominantly female? By Marie Glenn, March 2, 2017. https://www.ibm.com/blogs/insights-on-business/ibmix/good-men-growing-population-ai-voices- predominantly-female/

In Order Of Appearance:

Margaret Galey is an Iowa-born artist and writer living in Lexington, Kentucky. Her work has appeared in publications such as Hyperallergic Weekend, Druken Boat, and more can be found on her website: www.WantReaction.com.

Danielle Vermette is an actor, a freelance writer and a dog walker living in the Pacific Northwest. She wrote and directed her first play, "Dear Marna" which opened at Imago Theatre in January, 2019. She studied in the Portland State MFA fiction program and was a finalist (and the Oregon winner) of the 2012 Wordstock fiction contest. She writes regularly for Oregon ArtsWatch and occasionally reviews poetry for the Oregonian.

Olivia revels in anachronisms—of shooting film in the 2000s; of writing fiction in the age of viral videos. Her interest in space is translated into a photography that seeks out light and void, absence and inertia, particularly in a world that can often be crowded in its own chaos.

Kryston currently resides in New Jersey, but her heart and her home are in Texas. She writes poetry while on the train to her job at a boutique wine shop in NYC.

Maegan Gonzales is a multi-disciplinary artist who bleeds out on blank sheets of paper, cardboard, clay, or whatever material she can find. She is currently based in southwest Louisiana where she lives with her family and cats, propagates plants, teaches yoga and English, and is pursuing her MFA in Creative Writing at McNeese State University.

Valyntina Grenier makes art on the side of life that insists, "Don't Shoot." Her poetry and visual art push the boundaries of representation and abstraction to create a vantage from which to view violence and prejudice. Her work has appeared or is forthcoming in, Lana Turner, JuxtaProse, Cathexis North West Press, Bat City Review, The Volta's Arroyo Chico and Spiral Orb. Her first chapbook Fever Dream/ Take Heart (a double) is due out January 2020 from Cathexis North West Press. Find her at valyntinagrenier.com or Insta @valyntinagrenier

Phoebe Millerwhite is an artist and writer living on the outskirts of Los Angeles. She has degrees in Writing, Literature, and most usefully, Folklore. Her nonfiction has appeared in The Los Angeles Times. Once upon a time Phoebe was the manager of an art gallery.

Based in Los Angeles, Christine Friedman specializes in watercolor paintings, oils and collage. Her paintings speak to memory, chronic pain & current events. Her works have been sold internationally and have appeared in multiple shows. IG: @girlcabart

In the past, Stacey has taught college composition and literature for 13 years in Southeast Missouri, but she moved in 2012, with her husband and son, back to St. Louis where she continues to write, teach, and lecture at the college level. She has taught almost 20 years at the college level and enjoys being in the classroom with her students.

Samantha Madway is working on a collection of interlinked poems and flash fiction. She loves her dogs, Freddie, Charlie, Parker, Greta, and Davey, more than anything else in the universe. Her writing has appeared in SLAB, Sky Island Journal, unstamatic, Flexible Persona, After the Pause, Maudlin House, and elsewhere. She's technophobic but attempts to be brave by having an Instagram @sometimesnight. If the profile were a plant, it would've died long ago.

Natasha Moskaljov is a Croatian writer, former dancer and yoga teacher with a degree in Economics currently based in Spain. With interest in anything deep, she explores layers underneath the daily and the obvious.

Cindy Sams is a writer and teacher from Macon, GA. She is pursuing an MFA in Creative Writing from Reinhardt University in Waleska, GA. She specializes in Creative Non-Fiction with a particular interest in place.

Barrie Stark is a self taught watercolorist since 2016. She also paints in oils, acrylic and (also self taught) soft pastel. She paints from her heart and intuition. Not happy with a piece unless it has bright happy colors, and maybe a small bit of moodiness, as that perfectly describes her personality. This series is an ongoing sketchbook project. Her plan is to keep all of these in the book and not release them for sale, until the book is complete. We'll see what happens...

Gina WIlliams is a Portland, Oregon-based writer and artist. Ginas writing and visual art have been featured most recently by River Teeth, Okey-Panky, Carve, The Sun, Fugue, Palooka, Boiler Journal, Whidbey Art Gallery, Black Box Gallery, and Great Weather for Media, among others.

Elena Tomorowitz earned an MFA from Cleveland State University's NEOMFA, and PhD from The University of Southern Mississippi's Center for Writers, both with a focus on poetry. She has work appearing in Guernica, The New Guard, Hayden's Ferry Review, Fugue, The Collagist, and others. She lives in Boise.

After thirty-five years of teaching mathematics and leading schools, then retiring from the daily life of school but not from thinking about teaching and learning, Joan Countryman has turned to writing poems. Poetry for her is a lot like mathematics: a way of making sense of the world. She wishes the discourse on education were more about democracy and less about saving money. She believes that the future of every country depends on access to strong public education for all children. In her poems the child who read ahead in the reader, the sixties activist turned teacher, the mother and grandmother, the seeker, records insights and memories, fancies and dreams of a future of justice for everyone.

Karyna Aslanova is a Kyiv-born Ukrainian multimedia artist, director, and photographer. Karyna studied Theatre Directing at The National Academy of Government Managerial Staff of Culture and Arts, Kyiv, Ukraine and although photography is her principle medium, Karyna also uses video, painting and illustration, and poetry to further her exploration into a multitude of subjects. Karyna's art photography projects often use other-worldly imagery to reflect modern social issues, with a vague but familiar base note perceptible through a haze of the strange and incongruous.

Julia Muench is a visionary multi disciplinary artist, designer and innovator in the arts. She has a large body of visual and sound work. Some of her work may be seen at artwork archive:
https://www.artworkarchive.com/profile/julia-muench
Julia grew up in Miami, Florida, taking art classes (drawing and sculpture) at a very young age. Her mother, Deborah Winter, an artist in her own right, introduced her to art at an early age.
Later though still trained and working in art, Julia decided to go on study music and received her Master's degree from the University of Miami School of Music.
Julia 's initial fascination for the esthetic in geometry started sound-wise with her career in music and composition, and then continued to manifest in her art quilts going back to 2006. Since that time, Julia has continued to develop her own designs expanding into other media such as mosaic and sculpture.
Julia is an experienced artist, performer, musician, composer, and educator, has won achievement awards for her art quilts, music performance, teaching, and sound compositions. She has also studied and performed and choreographed various dance forms such as flamenco, and worked in film and photography.

rlongfield was born in Chamblee, Georgia, but was raised in the small town of Midway City, CA. She has lived in the Inland Empire for several years. This is where she and her husband John raised their two beautiful, amazing daughters. She cannot remember not being a writer or wanting to be a writer. She loves making people laugh, but is now often sad that current events provide her with so many opportunities to skewer the present powers that be. Or want to be. She is very grateful for the understanding of her husband John, and her daughters, and the support of her family and friends.

Kelly O'Rourke received her MFA in Creative Writing with a concentration in Poetry and MA in English at San Francisco State University. She has published poems in HCE Review, The A3 Review, The Hong Kong Review, Crab Orchard Review, South Florida Poetry Journal, Red Earth Review, Slaughterhouse Magazine, Poet's Haven Digest, Snapdragon Journal, Transfer Magazine, Holy Sh*t Journal and Blue Collar Review.

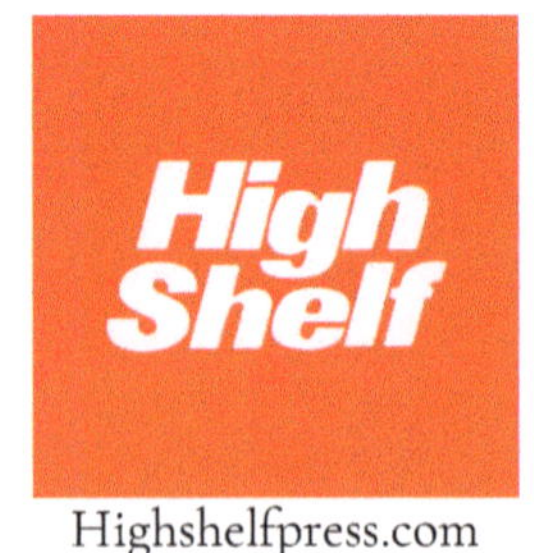

Highshelfpress.com

www.ingramcontent.com/pod-product-compliance
Lightning Source LLC
Chambersburg PA
CBHW050037040726
47599CB00015B/1718